Mayan Astrology

Ancient Wisdom

For Your Sun Sign

& Compatibility

By Yuriria Robles & Nadiya Shah

Copyright 2021

Published by Synchronicity Publications

All Rights Reserved

ISBN: 978-0-9947559-6-4

Yuriria's Dedication:

For all those who love the sky and its wonders.

Nadiya's Dedication:

Dedicated to my Fabulous Friends, Fans, Superstars, and Students. Thank You for seeing me as a part of your sacred journey, as you are part of mine.

I am grateful.

Disclaimer: This book in no way provides medical advice. The author and publisher advise and encourage seeking professional, medical advice, insight, and assistance for any and all ailments or questions, physical, psychological, or otherwise.

Table of Contents

Forward By Nadiya Shah	7
Introduction	11
The 13 Signs	19
Snake - Kan - Wisdom	21
Rabbit- Túul-Sensitivity	29
Turtle- Aak- Patience	35
Bat- Zoots- Family	41
Scorpion- Dsek- Discrete	47
Deer- Ceh- Conciliator	55
Owl- Moan- Seer	63
Turkey - Kutz- Traveler	71
Alligator Gar- Xibcay- Investigator	79
Monkey- Batz- Changeable	85
Falcon- Coz- Intellect	93
Jaguar- Balam- Protector	99
Dog- Pek- Loyalty	107
Compatibility	115
Snake, Kan	117
Rabbit, Túul	119
Turtle, Aak	121

Bat, Zoots	123
Scorpion, Dsek	125
Deer, Ceh	127
Owl, Moan	129
Turkey, Kutz	131
Alligator Gar, Xibcay	133
Monkey, Batz	135
Falcon, Coz	137
Jaguar, Balam	139
Dog, Pek	141
Acknowledgments and Gratitudes	143
Credits	146

Forward

By Nadiya Shah

I first met Yuriria way back in 2013. I was invited to attend an astrology conference in Mexico City, and bring my show *Synchronicity WebTV,* to interview some of the brilliant people presenting there. When I see these interviews I giggle to myself. I was so determined to speak Spanish! So many generous people told me my Spanish was good. I look back, and now that my skills have improved, I can't say I agree with them. Though I am grateful for the time shared with me.

One of the presenters was Yuriria. I approached her for an interview, and was delighted that she spoke English. I quickly felt an admiration for her brilliance, and an energetic connection. It was as if I found a soul sister. She told me that she was the only astrologer who worked for the Mexican government. She mentioned how she worked to bring astrology to the National Lottery. She had seen me post the very lottery tickets she worked on, on my Instagram account, just weeks earlier. This and many more moments made it clear we were connected.

Over the years, this connection has only fortified that much more. She is one of the very few people who has seen my astrology chart, who provides me with insights that are uniquely hers and that also bring me a sense of healing and release. She has appeared on my YouTube channel a few times, because she is just that good. I have loved hanging out with her on camera and off. We have had countless meals together, and spoke endlessly of all the ways in which we could work together. And now, here we are.

It was always a part of my vision for Synchronicity Publications, that I would one day have other authors on my label. Authors that I believe in, that I want others to know about, that I believe have wisdom, knowledge, and insights that need to be shared with the world. How fitting, and what a privilege for me, that Yuriria is the first author, other than myself, that I get to present to world.

This book is divided into distinct sections. The first is the introduction, and it helps you to understand how the Maya saw and made sense of the zodiac, and the various cycles they had. The Second goes though each of the Sun Signs, helping you to quickly navigate to your own Sign, so that you can explore your animal totem, and see yourself in new ways. The third explores how the signs interact with each other. This section allows you to consider the relationships and alliances you have in your life, to understand them from the perspective of Mayan wisdom.

What I have done in this book is take the wisdom and brilliance of Yuriria, and put it into my own words. The knowledge and insight belong completely to her, as it should. She is a world renown expert in the topic. I took the translation and, with her complete permission, added my own flare. In this way, I feel that this book can be made that much more accessible to that many more people. And this wisdom should be out there. It needs to be known by as many people as possible. It is that valuable, that useful, that beautiful.

By presenting this wisdom to the world, I feel like this is just one small way I can give back to my adopted home of Mexico. It is a land and a people that I love so much. Yuriria has helped me understand the spiritual roots to this land, the history extended back to its origins. We have spent countless moments discussing the rich traditions, historical phases, various indigenous groups of which the Maya are one, and psychological implications, of this beautiful land and its diverse people. Now, I get to be part of bringing some of this depth to a larger audience, and perhaps an audience that wouldn't otherwise understand how valuable this information is. I get to share the brilliance of my friend, but also affirm the love and wisdom of this very special place; Mexico and the intense, insightful knowledge of the Mayan people.

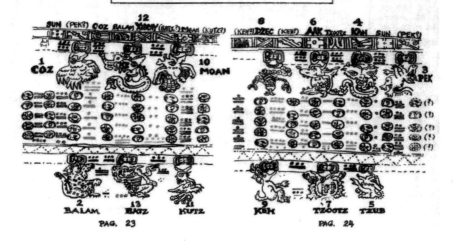

Restoration of The Table Of Eclipses, which illustrates the Mayan Zodiac
Paris Codex

Introduction

Star-Gazer, The Madrid Codex

The development of Mayan culture is an example of incredible human capabilities. The wisdom and insights they cultivated lead people to overcome the adversity of sometimes hostile terrain. This also gave them the ability to predict events, through a careful observation of the stars and the environment that surrounded them.

By studying the sky with depth, they developed a complete science that included astronomy, mathematics, meteorology, botany and medicine; all with the main goals of surviving and preserving their culture and knowledge. This legendary ability to understand time and space, based on a cyclical and spiral idea, helped them expect their rises and falls, and even their own resurgence. This ability for anticipation interrelated the stellar, solar, lunar and planetary cycles as indicators of the time and fate to come. Through this system, the Mayans blended the cycles of luck and fortune closely.

Prophecies were a regular subject among the Mayans, and were made by different priests called Chilam Balam (which means the prophet's mouth). This was the name given to those who made speculations about what they observed from the sky. They studied the sky, recognizing short and long complete cycles of the Sun, the Moon, the Planets, the Stars and even the Milky Way.

Their observations were recorded in types of books called codices, made of amate bark paper. However, only three remain to this day: The Paris Codex, The Madrid Codex and The Dresden Codex, named for the cities in which they are housed. These 3 works are central to the information presented in this book. This is where we find the Mayans' understanding of the cosmos, and the significance of each constellation, including the Sun Signs presented here.

Upon the Spanish arrival in the Colonial Era, a series of almanacs emerged, and were used to make these prophecies known. They were called The Books of *Chilam Balam*, or "Books of the Prophets." These books contained useful principles for daily life in the areas of medicine, the calendar, history, religion and, of course, predictions.

This wisdom reappeared at the end of the 19th century when Juan Jose Hool brought the *Chilam Balam* of *Chumayel* to Friar Crescencio Carrillo and Ancona. Another complete version is called *Maní*, which Juan Pio Pérez compiled. There are more versions that consist of almanacs and medical books, like *Tekax*, the *Chan Cah* and *Ixil*, all found in Yucatan towns. There are 17 books that were recovered.

The *Chilam* Balam books contain the prophetic Wheel of the *Katuns*, the Signs of the *Tzolkin* calendar, the *Haab* year and its meaning, the hidden *Suyua* language, astrological correlations, as well as festivities, ceremonies and remedies. In fact, the only things that are preserved from their traditions are inside these books, the rest are modern interpretations and observations.

Their prediction bases are divided into 4 cycles: Their prediction bases are divided into 4 cycles: around the days, the months, the planets, and the constellations.

In understanding your Mayan Sun Sign, we look to the constellations. It is this cycle that speaks to key characteristics your Sun Sign holds, depending on what constellation you were born under. It is from this place that we will now explore each of the Mayan Constellations, and their significance to.

Original Copy of The Table Of Eclipses, which illustrates the Mayan Zodiac
Paris Codex

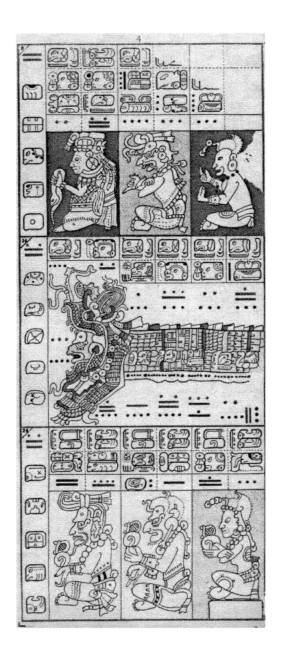

Representation of the Milky Way, Planets, & Directions
Pg 4 & 5 of the Dresden Codex

The 13 Signs

Snake - Kan - Wisdom

May 4th to May 31st

The fact that the Snake is the Mayan symbol of life and its cycles are based on the extraordinary relationship that indigenous people found in the biology and behavior of the Snake. They saw a correlation between the habits and movements of the Snake, and celestial cycles, with the development of life and the movement of the sky.

The Sun, the Moon and the Planets rise and fall in the firmament as a winding Snake in the Sky. The correlated this to the ways in which the Snake itself will emerge and return to below the surface of the Earth. Every day the Sun crosses the sky in a continuous swing of sunrises and sunsets, but each day is different in position and altitude. This was something they were not only aware of, but followed with great care and detail, feeling a profound connection with the Sun and all the planets. They built large and small observatories, which followed the solar direction, recorded the day as the basic unit of their calendar and tracked the light of each day of the year, from dawn to dusk.

The Moon also crosses this path marked by the Sun in a wavelike pattern, moving further north and south than the rest of the planets. Although the planets also ascend and descend in this celestial Snake-like movement forever, on its way, the Sun is joined by groups of stars that, as a whole, create a circle of animals, and are fundamental in the Mayan culture for their magnitude and power.

In addition, the Snake's rattle resembles the soft pitter-patter of the rain in the jungle. The beginning of the rainy season also marks the beginning of the Mayan Zodiac, which forms a ring that twists on its own and starts over.

The Snake's regeneration capacity reaffirms the myths of the eternal return and recurring cycles which were the center of the Mayan belief, realizing that inside the human body and in the wavy movements of human physiology, there is a Snake that undulates and it is related to men as a link between these two worlds. Assuming he is capable to integrate and understand that life is full of cycles that have to be celebrated, and accepting that it is necessary to transform and reinvent ourselves whenever possible. Even the Snake' skin design has a pyramidal shape, confirming the idea of the mountains and observatories. With each Snake scale, they counted the days, weeks, months, and years.

Habitat

They are poisonous Snakes endemic to the American continent, from southeastern Canada to northern Argentina. RattleSnakes (Crotalus) are a genus of the pit viper subfamily within the viper family. Called among the Mayans Tzab Kán, that is to say the rattle of the Snake.

All but one species, Crotalus catalinensis, are easily recognizable by the characteristic rattle on the tip of the tail and depending on the exact species, they have a slim and compact body. Their head is rather flat, and it's clearly noticeable from the neck. The center of the body is surrounded by scales that are arranged in 21 - 29 rows. The background colour of this family ranges from yellowish to greenish, or reddish to brown, and even black. A row of dark rhombohedral spots run down the back and sides.

Behaviour

They normally live in sandy forests and in coastal areas. Their skin, with yellow circles, is marked in the center by black colors. RattleSnakes are very high-strung animals, though individual temperaments vary. They are often easily excitable, and even seemingly docile species can attack abruptly without warning, so caution is advised. However, they only attack to defend themselves, and in dangerous situations. These Snakes roll up and put their necks in an "S" shape in order to attack quickly. With their tail, they emit a warning sound.

The Sacred This Month

During this time of year, The Mayans celebrated their rain deities. Some of these deities include the *Kuk Ik Kanes,* who are feathered beings of the wind. When the open star cluster Pleiades emerged shortly before sunrise, this became a symbol, announcing the season to start their rituals to rain deities. In this month, another deity, *Kinich Ahau* descends to ripen the seeds. The town of Edzná, in the state of Campeche, holds an ancient pilgrimage site. The main pyramid holds an image of *Itzamná* sowing, lit up at sunset, leaving the rest of the pyramid in darkness before the thousands of people who would gather in great groups, at this time of the year.

Sign Traits

★ The Snake is an animal of power, wisdom, and time. Those born in this period seek freedom to unfold the strength they possess. Their path towards becoming their best self may at times appear slow to others, but as they learn to tap into an authentic voice within, outer fulfillment and success follows.

★ Snake people carry great energy, but sometimes they don't know how to use it; If not careful and consciously directing their powerful serpent energy, they can be violent or hyperactive, and should practice great care in this regard. While this tendency isn't likely in most Snake people, they may need to learn to channel this powerful energy of anger towards its regenerative potential.

★ Snake people can be of great help to others, if they use this powerful energy for healing. They can direct the energy of life-force to those who are sick due to lack of energy. Practices such as Reiki, or other forms of intentional energy direction are powerful practices to help these people learn how to use this energy well.

★ Knowing the forces of nature is something natural in Snake people. They are careful merchants and have a good heart. Part of what makes them great at business is that they understand growth is not a steady, upward journey. There are cycles to any meaningful growth, that has its curves and dips. They also have an intuitive understanding that their goals are not only for the end, but also about the deeper emotional and spiritual lessons they learn about themselves along the way.

★ The animal Snake will shed dead skin at key moments. In fact, the Mayans routinely saw the dead shell that Snakes in the wild would leave behind, in their tracks. Similarly, Snake people will have key moments in life, when they are asked to release and regenerate, and to begin again. When they embrace this as an essential part of their journey, they find these to be exciting times, filled with the spirit of life and change. When they resist times that ask for evolution, they make it infinitely harder on themselves, experiencing emotional turmoil and feelings of loss. Attitude and perspective changes the experience of change itself.

Message

The Snake's journey is that of self-trust in your instincts and your connection to the Earth. You can do this by consciously spending time with a feel of dirt beneath your feet. However, in all matters, you are able to connect to a natural instinct within, that encourages you to cultivate self-trust. From there, you're able to gain maximum personal strength to reach the heart of the sky.

In Love

These types can fall in love easily and might constantly seek not to be alone. They have a drive towards intimacy and closeness, but are also aware that with intimacy can come complex feelings and emotions. They might appear demanding and jealous at times. However, this often arises from an awareness of their own ability to love more than one person. These emotions might also be rooted in fear of rejection, in the face of emotional intimacy.

They can handle being in two relationships, and might defend the choice. However, when they are monogamous they are completely immersed in the other, giving their whole selfs to the bond. They need gentle and sensitive partners, who will honor their sometimes complex feelings and emotions. They are sensual and down-to-earth in love. To keep their love relationships, they must accept their needs, being able to give and receive pleasure, freeing themselves from possessiveness.

Rabbit - Túul - Sensitivity

June 1st to June 28th

For the Mesoamerican, the Rabbit was a soft and light animal, which escaped from almost every predator chasing it, and could then easily disappear into its burrow. It was as fertile as the Moon goddess, and they noticed the shape of a Rabbit on the lunar surface.

Rabbits are ancient animals. Fossil studies have determined that before the last glacial period they were already present. Most Rabbits are native to North America, Europe, and Asia, and they live almost anywhere, including forests, grasslands, deserts, and tundras.

Leporidae (Leporidae, from the Latin lepus, hare), popularly known as Rabbits and hares, is a family of lagomorphic mammals that include 11 genera and over fifty species.

They have an athletic build, with robust, well-muscled back legs that allow them to propel themselves with speed, performing impressive jumps and acroBatics. The tail usually has the ventral area clearer than the rest of the body, so they can make rapid movements. Sometimes Rabbits stomp their hind legs down onto the ground, expressing anger or annoyance. When they are happy, they grind their teeth to show enjoyment and pleasure.

Mating

Rabbits are usually a symbol of fertility because of their great reproductive capacity and for the same reason, they also represent the time when cycles begin and earth becomes fertile. It has been calculated that the offspring of a single pair, without negative interferences in their development, can reach the incredible number of 1, 848 litters! The role of the Rabbit as prey also lends itself as a symbol of innocence, since it is an animal that doesn't seem to have the intention of hurting anyone.

The Rabbit and Its Ears

According to Mesoamerican mythology, once upon a time, the Rabbit had tiny ears. They were as small as the ears of a kitten. The Rabbit was happy with its ears, but not with the size of its body. All the animals chased it or defeated it, so it went to see *Itzamná*, the great God. As soon as it spoke with God, it asked him to make it very big. *Itzamná* asked the Rabbit why did it want to be big? The Rabbit said that only then it could defend itself from everyone. However, to grant its wish he tested the Rabbit: It would have to do three difficult tasks. God asked for the skin of a crocodile, of a Monkey, and of a Snake.

The Rabbit, besides being cunning, mischievous, and cheerful, liked to play tricks on other animals, big and small. They were fond of entertaining all animals equally, and had many friends. Their stories frequently depict the Rabbit as social and attending festivities and parties.

The Rabbit found the crocodile first and asked if he could borrow its skin without giving explanations. The crocodile assumed the Rabbit would use it to go to a celebration. Later the Rabbit visited its Snake friend, which also agreed to let it borrow its skin. The Monkey did the same. Everyone thought the Rabbit was going to a fun party.

The Rabbit went back to *Itzamná,* who was surprised, but realized how smart, clever and graceful the Rabbit was. *Itzamná* touched its little head, and at that moment, the Rabbit's ears got larger than its body. When the Rabbit saw them, it was grateful and left jumping. *Itzamná*, rather than making the Rabbit bigger, gave it a good sense of hearing, so it could protect and defend itself from predators approaching.

Sign Traits

- ★ The Mayans believed that Rabbits were symbolic of the power to make and stop rain from the sky. Rain being symbolic of life, fertility, calm, and richness, the mayans understood that, just like the rabbit, these qualities can feel fleeting at certain times in life. In this way, Rabbit people too understand that life can jump from one state to the next, at times feeling calm and secure, at others being more variable. These types can find joy and peace in it all.

- ★ Rabbit people can be shy, but are fond of a laugh. They are keenly aware of their mystical and rebellious sides. They might sometimes feel misunderstood, but an inner connection to source keeps them confident of their strength and character.

- ★ Rabbit people can become good guides to others, with an instinctive understanding of the best places to go to get just about anything. This can be related to physical places, such as tour guides to their home town and faraway places. This can also be a guide in spiritual and mystical matters, helping others in their journey through life. They help others more than with just their words, but also with their courage to act.

★ Rabbit types are by nature inclined towards being foragers and vegetarian eaters, with a highly developed instinct, linking the earth and the forces of nature. This shows up in how they utilize all of their senses, though what stands out is Rabbit peoples' sense of hearing. It is usually exceptionally keen and well-developed.

★ Rabbit people can be elusive. They are hard to catch, literally and figuratively. They know how to flee from danger, and the forces of nature have an uncanny way of protecting them. The Rabbit finds greater peace as they move through life, once they learn to trust their inner guidance, and the real protection offered to them in the natural world.

★ Rabbit people must make their way in all things, including in life. They hold an innate desire for independence and self-determination. They thrive on the feeling that comes from knowing that they can take care of themselves, financially and otherwise. Rabbits must learn to stay open to the energy of the rain. They thrive on the feeling that comes from knowing that they will be all right, whether alone or with another. They are especially adept and happy when staying in tune to the never ending Zodiacal cycle, whether this comes through practices like astrology, or through observing the powerful ways in which synchronicity plays out in their lives.

Message

Listen carefully to the voice within your heart, but also to the messages that life tries to send you. A part of you needs to feel constantly light and free, and you can have this, while also holding responsibilities that are meaningful to you. Stay flexible as you tap into what you are passionate about, in every area of life. It is in listening to and trusting your passions, that you find yourself living a life that feels especially rewarding.

In Love

They are absolutely loyal, seizers of opportunities in love, and they pursue their passion. They are very affectionate and friendly. Some may have excessive demands of their partners, which might be tempered by having passions in life outside other relationships to pursue. They usually have large families, and love to indulge in festivities and celebrations. Their challenge in romantic relationships is to overcome the temptations that lead them to believe in intentions and illusion. Love that is practical and real can still be vibrant and fun.

Turtle - Aak - Patience

June 29th to July 25th

Mexico is undoubtedly the country where more species of Turtles come ashore to spawn, than most anywhere else in the Americas. Mexico receives 7 of the 8 species of sea Turtles in the world, including one species, the Kemp's Ridley Turtle, whose nesting occurs almost entirely in Mexico.

Turtles, or chelonians, are a type of reptile characterized by having a broad and short trunk-back, and a shell that protects the internal organs of their body. Turtles cannot remove their shells, because their spine and ribs are welded to it. Like all reptiles, Turtles are ectothermic animals, so their metabolic activity depends on the external or environmental temperature. Turtles shed their skin; however, unlike lizards and Snakes, they do so little by little, so as to be almost unnoticeable to those who observe them. They also shed the shields from their shell, individually and without a particular order.

Duality and Patience

In warm climates, all species of Turtle hibernate regularly. They are oviparous animals, and they lay their eggs in nests they themselves dig in the ground, where heat is provided by solar radiation. Their metabolism is very slow. Aquatic species can remain without breathing for a long time.

They are a symbol of duality, because they are very slow at walking on the Earth, but they are great travelers in water. Its ancestral memory is one of the oldest, and it has witnessed the evolution of the species on this planet. Mayan wisdom states that the map of the celestial vault is printed on their shells.

The Mayan worldview establishes a deep relationship between the behavior of the stars and that of animals. A relationship that was later incorporated to explain human psychology. In the

Turtle's case, the Mayans saw a rich symbol that embodied the initial substance, that of which all living beings are made from.

The slow gait of the Turtle can be seen as perseverance, as building life little by little, like the Sun's motion in the sky that forms the shape of a Turtle on its way, in analemma, forming the infinity symbol in its movements. The central temples of *Uxmal* and Old *Chichén Itzá* show elements of this little animal.

Sign Traits

★ Turtle people create a homey, nurturing, and peaceful feeling wherever they go. They might appear to go slowly through life, without haste and without frights, knowing the journey is all their own. Intuitively, the know that life is to be taken at their own pace, and no one else.

★ Turtles are normally conservative in nature. They like to honor traditions with strong family roots. They will adhere to customs and ritual, follow authority, display good manners, strong ethics, and core human values. They abide by the rules naturally, and prefer the sense of structure it provides. In the family role, they are patient and loving with all. They represent the grandmother archetype in all of their bonds.

★ Turtle types have a deep religious sense and a great faith in a Higher Power. They might base most actions and life choices in the stability their faith brings.

★ Turtle people are smart and sensitive, but prone to frustration. These 2 personality traits might find a difficult time getting along, which only adds to their uncertainty. They key is to find a way to blend intelligence with their high emotional acumen. Once they find the right middle ground, Turtle people find their journey easier to engage, and more joyous.

★ Turtle people are persevering and diligent, and they know this is the way to achieve everything they set their minds to. They don't believe in easy results. They can develop their patience, knowing that eventually they will fulfill their goals as a natural result of trusting their own instincts.

★ A sacred part of the Turtle person's path is to keep moving. There is a deep, unconscious knowing of their own individual destiny. Their conscious understanding of their life purpose might feel illusive to them at times. Regardless of how connected they feel to where they are heading, they have the gift of forward momentum, and as a result end up in remarkable places, with enviable success.

★ Turtle types can be very sensitive, but also determinedly persistent. They have the ability to continue with great, inspiring personal fortitude, nonstop until they achieve their goals. Regardless of where they start, Turtles build their life little by little, on their own terms. Key moments in life are defined by the uncanny ability to escape from risky situations, just in the nick of time.

★ Because they are dual beings, they can be rude and get angry. They need to be careful to wield their anger with consciousness, or they might inadvertently cause callous hurts, especially for themselves.

★ Turtle people are protective and patient people. They will rarely use weapons, other than their strong shells, in which they hide so that the world does not attack them. In this way, their most important form of protection is in isolating themselves when they need to remember a more essential power within.

★ Turtles are the storytellers of the Mayans. Whether detailing historical recounts of true occurrences, or imaginative, visionary stories, they utilize their vivid imagination to make any story come to live. They have a way of conveying information in ways that make it real, and resonate with many. When they do tell a story, people remember it for a long time, if only for the entertainment value.

Message

Just as the Maya believe that the shell of the Turtle holds the stories of the entire history of life, you too collect wisdom in your path, and find unique and individual ways to share it. Your imagination is a great gift, as is your ability to remember certain essential truths about the human, or sentient, experience. You can use your most visionary sense to weave an image for a more wise and loving future, that you can diligently move all of humanity towards.

In Love

Take your time, in courtship and in romance. Turtles are patient, but the people in their life need to be patient with them as well. Their gift is the emotional connection that only they can offer, and that can take time to build. In love relationships they last a long time, even in the seduction phase. Therefore, they must be careful not to frustrate or rush to meet the expectations of their potential partner. That might lead to a lack of interest and exhaustion on the Turtle's part. Instead, if you desire the love from a Turtle person, trust that it will grow at the right pace and time. There's no need to hold your life or do anything different. Love with Turtle people is only if it's meant to be.

Bat - Zoots - Family

July 26th to August 25th

Chiroptera or **Bats** are an order of mammals with their forelimbs adapted as wings. With approximately 1,100 species, they represent approximately 20% of all mammalian species, making them the second largest order of this class (after rodents).

Bats are at home on all continents, except Antarctica. They are the only mammals capable of flying, and they have spread almost all over the world, occupying a great variety of different ecological niches. They are frugivores, surviving almost entirely on fruits.

Bats play a vital ecological role as pollinators and in seed dispersal; many tropical plants completely depend on Bats for propagation and continued reproduction.

In the Yucatan Peninsula, we find all Bats' species, insectivores, frugivores, carnivores and even hematophagous that feed only on blood. Most are nocturnal or active during the twilight period, and when they rest during the day, they need a safe place that offers them protection from the sun and rain, as well as from predators.

Bats are very important vertebrates in neotropical rainforests, constituting between 40 and 50% of the mammalian species in these ecosystems, but they also play a vital ecological role as pollinators. Many tropical plants completely depend on Bats.

Behavior

Bats have a sonar system that allows them to perceive their environment and, with insectivorous species, it also allows them to locate their prey. Contrary to myth, Bats aren't completely blind. Besides their sonar system, they use their eyesight for direction and locate their prey, or limit the area to return home. Also, Bats have a great sense of smell.

Revelatory Symbolism

Bat worshiping in pre-Hispanic Mexico dates back to at least 500 years BCE. Their representations include sculpted stone, ceramic urns, paintings and codices. Bats, or *zotz* as the Mayans knew them, were associated with populations and even calendrical times. Their image was directly connected to the underground world, with forces linked to earth, rebirth and death as opposed to the ideas of light, heaven and life.

The *Camazotz* or "death-Bat", among the Quiche Mayas, was associated with decapitation, which is symbolic of the death of passions, and the path from darkness to light. Through this process, the human soul, like the Bat, had to meditate for some time, recognizing its blindness and deprivation of power. When clarity came to its spirit, it could realize who it was and who was on its side. That is why the Bat is a clear representation of transformation and death coupled with the idea of a rebirth.

For the Mayans, it was fascinating to see an animal that moves through life at night, in the darkness. That's why in the symbolic world, but also in their lives, the Bat became a guide to enter and exit caves, and to walk in darkness, making the Bat a symbol of revelation as well.

This time of year celebrated divinities *Tzotz* and *Tzec*. Their descent to the underworld is celebrated at this time of year, marked by the cultural rite of 9 nights and days of fasting, until the change of the moon. After these 9 days, it is said these Gods emerged from the house of Bats, with profound wisdom to share with humanity.

Sign Traits

★ Most Bat species that are active at night share the ancient misunderstanding of how they could "see" in the dark. Guided by their sonar system or radar, they avoid bumping into things and stay away from obstacles that appear on the way. Their heads are always oriented towards the dark, where stars shine.

★ As a mysterious animal associated with darkness, the Bat represents the autumn equinox. The Bat is a symbol for those who seek or those who research, but also those who might be misunderstood and indecisive.

★ Bat people know how to guide themselves by their feelings and their intuition, which are very awake by nature, and especially awakened in natural settings. They have great ideas and can believe in what others do not. Bat people are especially attracted to paranormal events. Moments that represent the unknown being realized are especially intriguing.

★ The Bat is the symbol of a shaman, strong in character and with group instincts. They are people who gather for various purposes, whether for spiritual work, or in professional environments. Their professional lives might often involve the esoteric arts, whether directly or indirectly.

★ Bat people have a knack for solving problems and conflicts, or simply getting out of sticky situations in unexpected ways. They are adventurers, and might choose professions that engage this spirit, or rope in their fellow workers for some unofficial, joyous experiences.

★ The Bat has an innate spirit of curiosity, questioning and research. This is the case for all those born under this sign. Their nature is instinctive and they might, at times, act impulsively, doing what their instincts tell them to do. True wisdom comes when they gather enough experiences to hedge their bets, as to the most effective outcomes to their actions.

Message

The inner light is strong, and requires your self-trust. That light within you is there to be of service to others, to help them listen to their own inner voice. You are a natural guide, that can lead others out of some of the darkest times that people might face. Your own radar, and however you understand it, is usually on point, and should be something you lean on when you don't have all the details of a given situation. It will never lead you astray. Rebirth allows new foundations at many key moments, redefining your life again and again.

In Love

With characteristics of mystery, deep perception, and insight, these types bring these same characteristics to new people they might meet. They know how to listen, and they are patient and cautious. They can be very persistent during the seduction phase, but by taking deliberate slow steps, they quickly pick up on cues as to whether or not their advances would be welcome. Their sensitivity means that they would rather not risk with bold moves, that lead to rejection.

They usually meet their partners in groups or parties, preferring settings with low pressure, where they dont have to make their desire for love blatant. A part of them wants the instant pull of fate, wrought with intensity and demand. The intense emotions feel like love and passion to them. They can have very all-consuming love relationships, and might be possessive and demanding, until they face deeper feelings of vulnerability.

Bat people can be good partners with a parental drive, but sometimes it is hard to find out what they are really thinking about their spouse, or a matter related to a child. They strive to understand the inner workings of those around them, but might overthink certain behaviors. People very close to their heart might be perplexed at how the Bat person is constantly trying to find their deeper motivations.

Scorpion - Dsek - Discrete

August 26th to September 20th

There are some 1,400 species of Scorpions known worldwide. They reach body sizes between nine millimeters of the Typhlochactas Mitchelli, and twenty-one centimeters of the Emperors (Pandinus Imperator) or the Hadogenes Troglodyes.

They live on sandy or rocky soil, on tropical forests, or desert regions. A minority of them are climbing, vagrant, or cave-dwelling arboreal species. Some are synanthropic, accustomed to living around human beings and sustaining themselves through an informal relationship with us. Only a very few species of Scorpions are deadly.

Behaviour

Scorpions are a type of arachnids, with a pair of grasping pincers (pedipalps) and a tail ending with a stinger. They are the oldest known land animals. Fossils have been found in Silurian deposits, with an approximate age of 360,000,000 years. Their structure and form has changed little since then.

In Mexico, 104 species can be identified throughout the country. They are famous for their dangerous stings, and in Mexico 4 highly toxic species are known, although the power of the poison is highly variable among them, so it has always been advised to stay away from them.

It has been possible to identify that Scorpions have multiple senses; they are sensitive to the waves generated by the movement of their prey, and they have great chemical and light receptors. They also have well developed senses of touch, which they have perfected to high degrees, and it is essential for their survival. Within Scorpions, cannibalism is frequent, not merely because they are hungry, since they can store food inside their bodies, but it can be a prehistoric instinct that has taught them it is best to eat than be eaten.

Ancient Mythic Forms

Scorpions have played cultural roles for millennia. In myths and legends, they are often depicted as dangerous and deadly beings. They exist since the first human historical beginnings. Ancient inhabitants of the earth knew Scorpions well; In all languages and dialects of different tribes, there are words for them. Almost all storytellers mention them in their writings. They are usually represented as dangerous and deadly beings. However, they are also symbols of power and strength. They have played an important role in the imagination of different cultures for millennia.

The Mayans, the ancient inhabitants of the Yucatan peninsula, called them D*sek*, which simultaneously represents poison and medicine. Also, the Mayans had a deep admiration for an animal capable of withstanding the harsh climate, the scarcity of water and food. These traits represented worthy reasons for the Scorpion to be placed high in the sky, among the stars.

Scorpions are nocturnal animals that remain hidden during the day, for this reason they were associated with darkness, and similar to Bats, their constellations appear at dawn, during the time of the year in which periods of darkness increase, leading slOwly to the winter solstice.

For some historians, the behavior of this arachnid is like the development of Mayan history, in which relationships of great tension and fragility were established. Latent dangers among the dynasties of the great cities, in relation to the populations that were emerging, were always present. The tension led them to keep in close contact thanks to political, climate-related and geographical conditions.

Sign Traits

★ *Dsek* is the Mayan word synonymous for Scorpion. This is also the word for poison, and medicine, according to the dose and the way it is used. In the same way, power can kill or heal. This is a profound lesson that every Scorpion person comes to understand during at least one, key turning point moment in their life.

★ For the Mayans, those who were born under the constellation of the Scorpion were accomplished observers. Thanks to this quality, they could find the truth, which if told at the wrong time, could create problems. However, when the truth is told at the right time, it could be a force of healing, like medicine.

★ Scorpion people can be either overly controlled with their emotions, or short-tempered in nature. They rarely find a middle ground, especially in early life, instead vacillating between extreme emotional states. They might be afraid of expressing vulnerability of emotion, out of an instinctual fear of exposure, and the danger it inherently entails to their secret animal counterparts.

★ Scorpions are energetic people, who have a knack for moving towards, acquiring, and handling power. The Scorpion's luck has to do with looking for opportunities that arise, and responding quickly to take advantage of them. In this way, luck is often associated with timing, rooted in careful preparation.

★ The Mayans considered Scorpion people strong, with great agility and power, which they used for their survival. This was an especially valuable trait in the ancient world, where factors of fate could mean life or death in an instant. In the modern world, Scorpion people might use this energy to survive in professional environments.

★ Among their weaknesses, Scorpion were perceived as anxious, and sometimes unable to control their reactions. This shows in Scorpion humans, who have not worked consciously towards their evolution, in acts revenge and hurting others. This tendency can be overcome through consistent examination of ones own motives, and striving to align with higher principals of trust and assurance.

★ Scorpion people have great skills in starting and managing companies. They can also seem to be uncannily lucky. When a door closes, another opens for them rather quickly. This is an expression of how any ending brings with it a chance at rebirth, sometimes simultaneously.

★ There is a need to balance spiritual meaning and material desires. They like and need to live like kings, but what that means can be deeply personal. They might be at risk of losing a sense of proportion and spiritual reality, making it all about the material things. Humility is not their strength, although they admire and see it as a virtue, and might strive to achieve it as a well-earned personal characteristic.

Message

There are different types of truth; the subjective and the objective. Both are a precious gift, but can become skewed if not shared in a timely manner. Being sensitive to the needs to the moment, especially when sharing perhaps difficult truths, can be a skill that turns them into a force for healing. Also, being diligent in self-honesty, so that what opinion is not mistaken for fact, allows you to become more discerning in your delivery. It also strengthens your ability to transform and bring genuine medicine to any situation or moment.

In Love

Scorpions are animals without strong social ties, and only get close to another Scorpion during the mating season, a ritual in which they can end up being devoured by their mates. The human born in the Mayan month of the Scorpion might also feel the desire to devour a mate, with attention and physical connection. There might also be a fear of being devoured, of losing oneself in an intense bond. Their feelings can be complex and intense, at once wanting an all-consuming love, but also being frightened by the implications.

Those born under the sign of the Scorpion are stubborn and persistent in love, to the point of almost hypnotizing their partners. They are distrustful, and although they yield when they are seduced, they don't lower their guard. They like to live like kings or queens, so they demand to be treated as such, demanding a measure of respect from their partners. They have a strong desire to feel special to their partners in relationship. However, they are also willing to give it, wanting partners that they can share mutual respect with. If they choose to have children, they are very dedicated to them, to the point of sacrificing themselves for them. Their challenge is to learn to trust their partners by freeing themselves from the need to dominate, giving the relationship a deeper sense of commitment.

Deer- Ceh- Conciliator

September 21st to October 18th

Deer was valued as food, and was often part of rituals and offerings to the Gods. Preceded by the sign capable of withstanding scarcity, the Scorpion, we find in the Madrid codex the sign that shows abundance and one of the most precious delicacies for the Gods: the Deer. Even today it is considered rich people's food.

The white-tailed Deer is provided with small antlers and a tail under which there is a conspicuous white spot. Its potential habitat extends from Alaska to Bolivia.

Behaviour

Deer are slender herbivores with flexible and compact bodies, with long and strong legs adapted to move through forestlands and uneven terrain. Most Deer have a gland near the eye that has pheromones to scent-mark their territory. Males use these chemicals when they are bothered by other males.

Most Deer species live in family groups around a female. The gestational period for females varies between 160 days to 10 months. Depending on the species, they give birth to one or two fawns a year.

They feed on leaves, branches and plant sprouts. They are also excellent swimmers. The teeth of the lower jaw have raised enamel ridges, that allow them to crush a wide variety of plants. They are ruminants, herbivores surviving on planets, with a specialized digestive system. Deer have four-chambered stomachs, where food is digested.

Deer prefer the twilight hours, and can be in herds of 2 to 15 Deer. The basic social unit is a female and her fawns, the young males and the solitary males in the reproductive season.

When food is scarce, Deer approach the cornfields and damage crops. They have a fondness for corn, cabbage, peppers, pumpkin and melon, so orchards become the best places for them to look for food. In several states of the country, this animal was for many years the "headache" of farmers, because of the damage they caused to their crops. However, the farmers have been motivated to preserve the species, perhaps out of an ancient instinct, rooted in respect for the Deer, and still seeing them as a symbol of sacred prosperity. Even when considered pests, the Deer have been treated well.

The Deer's Antlers in The Madrid Codex

Males have antlers; which have several branches, but in the Mexican region of The Yucatan they have only two small antlers adapted to the type of vegetation. Because of this characteristic, the Deer was considered to have a special link between heaven and earth. It was associated with the ability to observe and understand celestial movements. It is likely the reason that this constellation is the most represented in the Madrid Codex, appearing 32 times in different tables, which documented the constellations and the rituals associated to them.

The first section in larger figures expresses the relationship with the previous constellation, the one of the Scorpion. This last sign showed the effort that the Mayan people had to make to survive, and the constellation of *Keh*—the Deer—was the prize, and it represented the abundance, as long as all the processes and works in the month of the Scorpion were done.

In the second section, in 14 squares and at first glance, the processes of hunting, distribution and offering achieved with the Deer were carefully detailed. In addition, the description of the movements of the Deer constellation, in relation to the constellations of the Jaguar, the hawk, the Snake and the polar star, among other celestial animals, was also defined.

The same happens in the Dresden Codex, where it shows on column 13 in front of the constellation of *Pek*, the dog; also within the tables of the planet Jupiter.

In a nutshell, the constellation of *Keh* symbolized an effort for structure, attention and sacrifice represented by the hunting process. By analogy, if we look through the antlers of the Deer, we find the astrologer peering, using a tool that extends towards the sky. Aided by branches of the highest trees in the peninsula, we can understand the usefulness of these elements in some of their temples as instruments of observation.

The month of the Deer was one in which the Mayan astronomers observed the sky and wrote the glyphs, arranging them to make the prophecies. For the reading ritual, they performed a dance called *Chan Tun Yab*, as part of connecting body and prophesy.

Sign Traits

★ Deers are hunted animals, therefore, they are usually nervous and methodical, restless but peaceful, territorial and adventurous, curious and shy. The Deer person's challenge is to achieve balance within these traits. To see them as part of a multi-faceted human experience is the first step towards self-acceptance. The next step involves finding the right balance, so these traits can be used to one's advantage.

★ Deer folks like to observe and integrate nature into their actions and choices. This gift towards observation can be used in formal pursuits, like astrology or astronomy. This internet might also be integrated informally, through paying attention to one's life, and learning through the experiences of others.

★ Deer people have strong, realistic paternal or maternal protective instincts, while keeping a hopeful, ephemeral energy in their approach to parenting. Like their animal counterparts, they live in family groups around a female. They are attractive and hopelessly attracted potential partners, believing that love is always possible.

★ Deer folks are elegant and stylish, in presentation and character. They also know how to navigate challenging situations both internally and externally, especially in interpersonal relationships.

★ Deer people are mild-tempered, although not always, as they react when threatened, through an outside observer may not know it. It can be easier for them to flee and hide than to confront the annoyances of confrontation or difficult emotions. They prefer to settle into their emotional currents, and only as a last resort will they confront another person.

★ Deer people investigate. They are disseminators, diplomats, rebels, often misunderstood and sometimes indecisive. Their challenge is to find the right balance. They are deeply in touch with sacred feminine energy, and show it through their ease of expression. They might find it difficult to adapt their soft and delicate ways to a world of aggressiveness, where demonstration of physical strength is prioritized. As such, they would do well in environments that allow them a full rage of emotional sensitivity and expression.

Message

Your sense of beauty and elegance inspire others. There is a natural grace that you hold, that allows you to turn situations of conflict into harmony or ease. However, the process might be an emotionally draining one. Still, engaging difficult moments might be worth the effort, as you discover new ways in which your light shines, and new things in yourself that you respect. Regardless of shyness or uncertainty, the effort it takes not to hide your light, helps it grow that much brighter. Listen to your inner wisdom in silence to learn the secrets of the Universe. They are all there within you.

In Love

Deer people can be happy either within a relationship or independently. There is a part of them that genuinely enjoys their own company. They are gentle and kind with their partner, but sometimes they are shy, out of fear of expressing too much emotion. They are docile and reserved, and don't impose heavy demands on their partner. They are tender, and when they are comfortable, they don't need seduction. However, they must set limits to avoid abusive relationships. Being overly sympathetic to others can lead them to make excuses for behaviors that shouldn't be excused. Deer like to integrate into large family groups, even to protect themselves. Their challenge is to show interest and attention to their partner, or to potential partners, knowing that they can express emotion and be ok whether it is accepted or not. Their gift is to create peaceful and harmonious situations.

Representation of the Owl Pg 10 of the Dresden Codex

Owl - Moan - Seer

October 19th to November 15th

Owls are great hunters, nocturnal and solitary. Owls are found throughout Mexico. They are amazing for their shape and behavior. It is not surprising that the Owls, Moan, or *Xoch* for the Mayans, were part of the emblematic animals of their Zodiac.

They are found all over the world except in Antarctica, Greenland, and some remote islands. Owls are birds from the order

Strigiformes. They are medium-sized birds, about 33 to 35 cm in length, and a wingspan of 80 to 95 cm, with an average weight for adults of 350 grams, and with no apparent difference between sexes.

The relatively short and rounded wings don't make it easy to have long and powerful flights. The particular structure of the Owl's wing feathers, especially soft and frayed, give them the ability to have a silent flight. When they are seen flying, it seems more as if they were floating rather than flapping. They are great hunters, but they are loners.

Behaviour

Owls feed mainly on small rodents, especially mice and shrews, although they also hunt small birds, insects and, to a lesser extent, amphibians and reptiles. Their hunting method comprises using their wide facial discs as sophisticated receptors to guiding sounds emitted by their prey, which they locate and catch with their long legs, pouncing on them in almost absolute silence.

They are considered the nocturnal eagles because they can see in the dark, and they understand the hidden activity of nature at night. Owls have the ability to skillfully fly and hunt in the different parts of the forest. The moonlight is their inspiration, and their singing is seen as either mysterious, inspiring, or frightening for superstitious people.

The Owl in The Dresden Codex

The presence and importance of the Owl is emphasized in the Dresden Codex, where its location and relationships with other celestial bodies are given.

Some interpret the Owl's sound as mournful and harsh. They also make a variety of different sounds, making it hard to identify what their intentions might be, except for the unmistakable hiss they make when they feel threatened or when their hatchlings ask for food. This is why the Owl drew the Mayans attention, and also why it has survived as a symbol. They announce, with strength, what is mysterious and bound to happen. Its unmistakable cry was considered clear and full of wisdom.

As their protector of nocturnal activity, the natives of Moan move in the dusky world, and for that reason they are associated with the messages of the sky. The Mayans attributed importance to them, and they gave them a month in the solar calendar. Their season was placed in May, when the growth of light transforms the sun into a more luminous bird, leaving the constellation of the Owl on the western horizon in the opposite direction to the sun at dawn, in the dark.

The Owl is also clearly shown in two temples. In *Uxmal*, in the rise called the Great Pyramid, where we can find a fresco with reliefs of Owls in all directions. In old *Chichen Itza,* where the Temple of the Owl is located to the south, it has symbolic representations associated with this bird.

This movement of the Owl constellation shows in both horizons. In the west during the sowing period, and in the east during the harvest period. This dual representation reflected the Owl's great intuitive power, and on the other, a clear and deep intellect. This granted the advantage to plan, study, and carry out their intentions to fruition. These two astronomical aspects, which place it in the east when the sun loses strength and the days get shorter, and in the west at the end of the year, allowed the Owl a greater presence among the Maya. The Owl guided over the entrance to the world of darkness. Its symbol remains that of an announcer of death. The Owl dominates the sky at a time of year when darkness increases, and represents the weakening of the sun.

The relationship of the constellation of the Owl with darkness also explains the strength of celebrating the traditional Day of the Dead during this period. These festivities continue under the light relationship of the sun and the earth. More interestingly, during the celebration in Yucatan called *Hanal Pixán*, words in the Mayan language that mean 'Food and Soul that gives life to the body', respectively, a dish called *Mukbil Pollo* (from the Mayan word *Muk*: bury and *Bil*: twist, stir) is made.
It is fascinating to know that the two particles together: *Muk-bil*, literally mean: "what has been or should be buried". To make the traditional dish *tamale*, a hole in the ground is made, where hot stones are used to bake. Nowadays, it is made with chicken or Turkey , but it is possible to speculate that this dish is the ancestral reference to the celestial bird of this period, the Owl,

that comes out of the darkness with messages from the underworld.

It should be noted that the ancient Mayans buried their dead in their backyards, since they believed they will hurt them if they weren't worshiped continuously. This special celebration for the dead during this period emerged during the Colonial era, but interestingly, the symbolic act of extracting the food for the soul from the underworld correlates to how the stars in the dark reveal their messages to us when we observe their light.

Sign Traits

- ★ Owls are night-birds associated with the wisdom of the sky. People born under this sign are stargazers and observers. They have intuitive faculties, inner senses and clairvoyant gifts.

- ★ Those born under the sign of the Owl between October 18 and November 14, like this bird whose eyes occupy 60% of their cranial activity allowing them to capture light even in full darkness, have the ability to look at what is dark and hidden. They are able to to recognize people's real desires.

- ★ Owl people success comes by being able to see what others cannot see, and to create strategies they carry out promptly. They can hear the slightest emotional subtlety of those around them, and can use this ability in all kinds of ways. Whether it is to gain a professional advantage among their counterparts, or to create stronger, more meaningful bonds,

★ Owl folks are seers and occult lovers, of both transcendental and fleeting doctrines. They know how to observe the stars and cultivate wisdom through their interpretations. They are intuitive, and see what others don't. Astronomy is an excellent hobby for them, as is astrology. The Owl will excel in any activity involving the deciphering of symbols.

★ Owl people might find themselves being very cautious or distrustful at times. As if they might be looking for reasons to justify their wariness. Their opportunity here is to see that people are complex, and to strive and see what could be good in what is less than ideal in us all.

★ Owl people have broad intellectual attitudes. They know how to take advantage of the night to plan, study, and carry out their purposes. In the quiet hours, they dream and achieve simultaneously, manifesting into reality what others might only dream of, but always with the goal of wisdom ever at the forefront.

Message

Responsibility and Wisdom are hard to gain, but the effort is often rewarded with treasures to be shared. The intuitive capabilities are very bright, leading to the ability to see what is otherwise hidden to most. Trust this inner vision, as it leads to the reveal of great mystery and occult knowledge. The emotional realities of life are strong, but can lead to powerful insights and learning, allowing for a richer experience of life than those of other animal signs might find. Part of the life path is to learn to separate emotional fears from spiritual truths. Once this fine balance is found, wisdom magnifies and grows that much brighter.

In Love

Owls tend to seek the truth in love, even if it means changing partners. They are serious to the point of shyness and sometimes reticence. They are good strategists, so they can have great plans to win their partner, whether their partner is in on it or not. In their relationship, they may come to believe their partner is their property. In this way, they might experience feelings of possessiveness, until they learn to choose partners that allow them the safe space to express, but not indulge, these feelings. When they feel secure with their partner, they usually form a stable sense of family. This is their best gift.

Turkey – Kutz – Traveler

November 16th to December 13th

Turkey or *Kutz*, as the Mayans called it in their language, is an endemic animal, native and unique to the region inhabited by this ancient culture. This bird is only found among the 130 thousand square kilometers that cover the Yucatan Peninsula, southern Tabasco, northeast Chiapas, Belize and northern Guatemala.

Long before the time of the Spanish colonization, and before the time that Europe learned of their existence, the Turkey was highly valued in everyday life for its tasteful meat. It was also considered sacred and honorable, holding its place among the Zodiac stars. It was given as an offering to the southern Sacred Mayan Tree.

Even today, it is highly regarded among the communities and local hunters in the Yucatan peninsula. The cultural process of domestication, used for several millennia, remains a key component in the ongoing relationship between the local indigenous people and the Turkey .

The Turkey is known for of its high nutritional value. It was listed as one of the most cooked animals in the kitchens of the region, but in recent years it has ceased to be so, since they were added on the endangered species list.

As a zodiac sign, the Turkey spanning from November 15 to December 13 is a symbol corresponding to the end of autumn and the regular dry season with night periods that are unavoidably lengthened.

The Turkey season emphasis the truth found in the inner Sun. The celebrated festivities at this time included *Olob Zab Kan Yax,* when people used body paint, to fashion themselves green and blue, to perform their flag rising ceremony.

Symbolically, the Turkey was considered similar to a Peacock. Both are confident, with bright feathers, and hold similar symbolism of beauty and pride.

Distinct Beauty

One of their most visually appealing features is their multicolored, bright and iridescent feathers. Precisely through this chromatic range of colour, females can be identified. Female feathers look more green and dully coloured. However, both sexes share primary and secondary wing feathers, which usually have a striped pattern. Their secondary feathers have a greater number of white areas, especially visible at the edges.

Turkey are surprisingly fast flyers. These colorful-feathered animals, native to the Mayan jungle, can be recognized by the blue color of their heads with orange or red spots. These fleshy spots found on the head are more protruding in males, and they are present on the upper limb and neck along with a ring of bluish bumps. This ring is extremely important for reproduction, because during mating season, it widens and its yellow-orange tints get more noticeable and prominent.

Mating and Breeding

The gobbling begins from the first rains happening in the last two weeks of March until the middle of May, with pre-adult males being the ones that stop gobbling first around this time.

Turkey are considered large birds, measuring between 70 and 90 centimeters. Its usual weight is three kilos for females and four for males. However, during the mating period, these numbers may increase.

Sign Traits

★ Like Turkey , those born during this season are aware of their beauty, and are innately sure of themselves. An essential part of themselves identifies as "attractive" or "unique". For people belonging to the *Kutz* sign, beauty and accessories truly matter, and their ability to attract others towards them, for personal or professional pursuits, remains strong throughout their lifetime.

★ Turkey folks might be shy as a first instinct, but will never let on, appearing self-assured in the way they present themselves. They and highly adaptable in any situation, and find ways to stand out as special, no matter the crowd. They feel an innate confidence, and they know they are valuable, even vitally needed.

★ Turkey people are cheerful people, with a sense of humor and optimism. These folks can see the best side of every situation. This attribute, and their charm, are appreciated and recognized by many. In many ways, it is this positive attitude that greases the wheels through life.

★ Turkey people don't get in trouble, and avoid conflicts as much as possible. They are patient with others, knowing that achieving personal growth takes time, and we are all going at our own pace.

★ Turkey folks need to shine and use their skills. They have a strong desire to be successful in some activity meaningful to them. They need to find, and value the purpose of their life, and it is reflected in the goals they set.

★ Those born in the Turkey month have intuitive and gentle skills. They instinctively understand the need to be careful with sudden outbursts of anger, so as not to put themselves in the way of physical harm. They can be graceful in neutralizing conflict.

★ The Turkey was given as a gift to those who needed to dominate their ego. It was a way of advising someone they didn't have to 'puff up' to show off, as male Turkey do during mating season. In this way, the human Turkey can seem egotistical. True influence comes when they understand their confidence can be a skill to move towards meaningful goals.

★ Turkey people know how to escape and move quickly, both physically and mentally, but they feel safe in intellectual environments, and prefer philosophical realms. They can be gentle and graceful, including in the exchange of passionate ideas and new thoughts.

★ Turkey people like to meet and coexist with their family group, and are able to do so without losing their individuality or their own desires. They are not one for wild parties, as gatherings might only heighten nervous energy.

Message

Healthy self confidence and self belief are great gifts. The key is to root these attributes in genuine confidence and faith. The risk is there that pride might be instead arising from a place of insecurity. Trust your unique beauty, because it truly is brilliant and impressive. You have special colors to share in this lifetime. As you grow older, and as you connect with inner vision and inner wisdom, you learn how to magnify your individual colors and strengthen your wings. Turkey truly do shine very brightly the older they get. The great gift of being a Turkey is the ability to gain attention for the higher qualities you love about yourself, and to be seen as a genuine, positive, and optimistic person, who spreads this optimism everywhere you go.

In Love

In love, they are affectionate and might have an almost uncontrollable hunger for love affairs. They need time establish courtship rituals, and to feel a sense of mutual appreciation, to feel attracted. Therefore, while they might feel an initial spark of desire, they want to see their potential love interest go through a type of performative and sometimes slow courtship, in order to allow the desire for each other to simmer and flow over.

Those born under the Turkey sign, although they fall in love a lot, prefer to be selective and create special conditions with their partners. Once they choose a partner, they like to implement a mutual teaching process. Just as Turkey perform a ritual to establish their bonds, those born between November 15 and December 13 need a special atmosphere to set them.

Giving love to Turkey means encouraging, cheering and reassuring them. They need to receive joy, trust and inspiration. They want someone who is truly on their side, and who sees them as special, desirable, and affirms their beauty. Once they feel this from a potential partner, they are able to give the same in return. Wanting recognition as a power couple might appeal to some Turkey . Mostly, they like the limelight, and want someone who will magnify that light, whether from on their arm or from behind the scenes.

Alligator Gar - Xibcay - Investigator

December 14th to January 10th

There are seven known species of Alligator Gar, and all of them are abundant in their habitats. The Alligator Gar is a predominantly freshwater fish, found only in North and Central

America; between Montana, southern Quebec and Costa Rica. Their habitat used to be much more widespread as evidenced by fossils found in Europe, Africa, South Asia and South America.

A fish that looks like an alligator because of its elongated and tubular shape, with a disproportionately large and elongated snout, although in some of its Lepisosteiformes relatives it is short, wide and shovel-shaped. Their skin is covered in a layer of hard diamond-shaped scales that create a kind of protective armor. The Alligator Gar has undergone virtually no change in the last 100 million years, which is why it is often considered a living fossil.

The Alligator Gar looks fierce and can be huge; some species reach almost 3 meters in length and weigh over 130 kilograms. Voracious and efficient predator, the Alligator Gar has a large mouth equipped with sharp, cutting teeth. Although it is usually a slow fish, it is also capable of sudden acceleration and it can swim at amazing speeds.

Behavior

The Alligator Gar generally remains motionless near the surface, drifting with the current and waiting for smaller fish to approach. As prey approaches, the Alligator Gar suddenly turns its head and grabs it, often from the side, then flips it over and swallows it in one bite.

One reason the Alligator Gar has survived for so long is because they thrive in rough waters. They have a swim bladder, that helps them gulp air when necessary, filling its gills with supplemental oxygen in environments where it is scarce.

Mating and Breeding

Reproduction takes place only in fresh water. The Alligator Gar mates between April and early June, and reproduce in early May to mid-June, in slow-moving waters with vast vegetation and low water depth.

A single large female can spawn with several small males. The eggs are green, toxic and very sticky. They adhere to the surface of aquatic plants, logs or underwater stones.

They grow fast, and their distinctive long jaw shows up quickly as well. During the first weeks of life, they remain very close to aquatic vegetation, until they can hunt by themselves and reach a considerable size to get away from their shelters. Their eggs are highly toxic to humans.

Sign Traits

★ Like this fish, those born under the protection of the Alligator Gar between December 14 and January 10 receive qualities that give them a deep capacity for survival, as well as an amazing aptitude for attention and self-protection. This serves them well in the unlikely situation of physical threat, but this tendency might have to be examined more closely when it is fear of physical closeness that motivates their self-protective tendency.

★ The time of year that the Alligator Gar represents is a time of great magic. This is when spiritual powers to sway the will of the gods was considered especially high, especially those with shamanic gifts and the skills to use them well. Similarly, Alligator Gar people can have great insight and understanding, able to move situations in their favor.

★ The Alligator Gar is an observer, and it prefers to hide than to face what it feels is a challenge. Its knowledge comes from these observation skills. It has a cunning, serene, as well as sharp and straightforward personality. They have the possibility of being in difficult environments, even toxic environments, and easily get out unscathed. The ability to make a decision, breathe, to recover and move on is one of their greatest personal gifts.

★ They are clever people, with the ability to make decisions that lead to success. They can be good entrepreneurs, because they know how to figure out the risks at starting businesses.

★ They can appear overemotional, but it is part of their charm. With an ability to be notably sympathetic to others, they are admired for forging genuine emotional connections and care with others. There are times when their temper can go overboard and others may dislike it, but that only happens in the cases where they feel there feelings are not being validated.

★ They can move as slow or as quick as the situation requires. This can be a physical feat, but is an emotional one as well. They are precise in their goals and rarely fail to achieve them. They wait for opportunities and once they feel ready, they act with precision. Their likelihood of successful outcomes is especially strong.

Message

You hold great strength of character, that might need careful observation as you learn to make the most of this personal fortitude. Some of your greatest gains, personally and professionally, come after a period of pause. These times, that seem like not a lot is happening on the surface, are a necessary part of the journey to meaningful success. Make the most of them by cultivating inner perception and patience with yourself and your life. You can see the subtleties that other might miss, making life that much more richly lived.

In Love

The Alligator Gar is capable of deep love relationships. They like active partners, so they will choose those they consider stronger and more powerful. The definition of these attributes is highly relative, and might not necessarily indicate a physical type. They are drawn to strength of character and those with a dynamic presence, who are comfortable with who they are and unabashed in showing it.

They are very patient, and can wait until they find a partner who they feel is the best for them. They might try many options, and go through periods where it seems they are dating many or no one at all. Their choice in someone to share their life with comes after consideration and time, taking into account all the ways in which this person adds to their life. It is never a solely emotional decision. They can also be patient with their partners. Being able to see nuances and complexities with the person they love, they might allow behavior that those outside the relationship can't always understand.

Those born at this time of the year, when the Sun is not hot, between December 14 and January 10, must recognize their need for affection and love by confidently opening their hearts to give and receive it. Love doesn't have to always make sense, and regardless of how much time was invested, it also doesn't need to last forever. The act of emotional exposure brings intrinsic rewards in the journey itself.

Monkey - Batz - Changeable

January 11th to February 7th

The Black Handed Spider Monkey is a native of the Americas (Ateles geoffroyi). It can be found in tropical forests, and in the light forests and dense jungles of Veracruz. They are also in the mangroves of Chiapas. They are in the many low jungle areas, and in the hummock forests, of Yucatan.

The Monkey also lives in lowland rainforests, gallery, and primary and secondary forests, but it can also live in high altitude forests from 250 to 1000 meters above sea level. It is also an important part of the great biological diversity of the jungle ecosystem in southern Mexico, where we can find Black Howler Monkeys (saraguatos) and Spider Monkeys.

Howlers feed on leaves, fruits and flowers of different trees. They are generally selective and they travel different distances daily in search of food. While Howlers only move several kilometers, the Spider Monkey, that only eats fruits, goes in search of food in a much greater area.

Monkeys can weigh between five and nine kilograms, and measure between 50 and 90 centimeters in length. A characteristic feature is their long, strong and prehensile tail, which they use as if it were just another hand.

Behavior

Monkeys of the region mainly feed on leaves, and make loud howls, which can be heard from 4.3 kilometers away. To make this sound, the Monkey will utilize a bony capsule, that inflates like a gallbladder, located under the tongue, and large laryngeal bags. This characteristic has also earned it the nick-name "Howler" by which it's popularly known.

The joint howl of large groups of Monkeys resembles the whistling of the wind, although much more powerful and sustained. They live in groups of three to seven Monkeys. These groups can have a single male or several. Each group lives in an area of 27 to 300 acres. It is actually the males of these groups, who are he ones that make these howls. This vocal behavior works also as a spacing mechanism between herds to avoid direct confrontations.

Magic and Memory

The month of the Monkey corresponded with rituals dedicated to the deities *Chén,* which translates to 'waterhole' and *Yax,* which means 'clarity'. These words together, represented a time dedicated *To recover the memory*. During this month offerings for renewal, to the *Aluxes* (mythical spirits) and *Yum Kax*, lord of the stars and the crops, were made.

Observing the Monkey quickly revealed how playful and mischievous they could be, with their counterparts in their community, but also with the people they came into contact with. Their physical agility reflected the ability to adapt and think quickly, with a constant sense that one could behave in ways unexpected or unplanned.

It is these very qualities of flexibility and adaption that came to be representative of youth and recovery. Whether this was to recover the wisdom of ancient memory for a new generation, or personal recovery and the memory of who one was at their essential self, it was the monkey that granted openness and happiness, to move you forward on a new journey, while grounded in useful memories of the past.

Sign Traits

★ Those born under the protection of the Monkey between January 11 and February 7, are skillful with their hands and playful. These qualities of play show up in many ways. Through the intellect or through behavior, there always remains a quality that is light. They can make even complex tasks seem like a joy

★ They have great mental dexterity and an extraordinary memory, almost eidetic. Their ability to learn quickly might need to be adapted to the skill of cultivating wisdom. There is a vast distinction between memory and wisdom, and yet, when they find the right balance, they become like the great historical wisdom keepers of the ages. This ability will likely take time, practice and age.

★ Because of their great mental capacities, they must be careful not to copy information. Their challenge is to develop originality. They might unintentionally plagiarize the work of another, but it truly is an unconscious act on their part. There is an inner drive to find their own uniqueness, just sometimes, they need it modeled for them.

★ Sometimes they can be perceived as "know-it-all", partly for the way they enjoy being able to remember in great detail what is hazy to others. This reputation might be one that is embraced.

★ Those born under the Monkey sign are usually loud-voiced. They need to realize that their voice will be heard far away, so they must take responsibility for what they say. Secrets will not likely be kept, by them or others. Information has a way of becoming public when Monkey people are involved. This can be used to their advantage, of course, especially when they are clear about what they desire to be 'heard' for.

★ The qualities that the Monkey brings to those born in this period gives them innocence, spontaneity and ability to play. They tend not to take things seriously. They like to laugh and make jokes. This ease can make them that much more a joy to spend time with, or even just be around. These same qualities make Monkey's popular in the company of others. Always being that easy going friend, with whom to share a spontaneous moment of joy.

Message

You have the ability to recover ancestral magic and memory. The latter comes more easily than the former. The ability to remember things can sometimes be taken for granted, because of how easily it comes. However, the magical part of them is always there. Many cultures have worshiped Monkeys, seeing in them something mystical and mysterious, and the fact that the Mayans recognized this as a time of ancestral magic suggests they too understood this archetypal correlation. This memory of magic is in you too. Overthinking can get in the way. Getting in touch with your ancestors, physical, spiritual, intellectual or otherwise, helps awaken this awareness of alchemy and chemistry, which makes life that much more meaningful.

In Love

Those born under the protection of the Monkey are very fond of affection and touching. They like having their partner close, and are quite literally hands on, in all kinds of ways. They can be just as affectionate in friendship, friends with benefits, or short term relationship situations.

Once they do find love, they are willing to make great sacrifices. In fact, love itself might be defined as inherently containing an element of atonement. When they know they are willing to give, to the point of considering their partner before themselves, that's when they know they are in love.

While they enjoy being pampered, they can do so without becoming submissive. In fact, they demand a sense of equality, the kind you would give to a friend or someone you see as the same as you. When they feel that they have this meeting of minds, they are that much more able to accept the adoring affections of another. And their partners know that they are also willing to give the same and they desire to receive.

The darker side of the Monkey's love reality is possible boredom, lethargy, or irritation within long term relationships. Their challenge to keep their relationships is to overcome their lack of inspiration and their extreme irritability. Keep life interesting, including in ways outside of the relationship. These can be platonic or intellectually driven pursuits. However, if they feel their partners lacking genuine understanding or friendship, they may start to consider what other options could be possible for them.

In their natural environment, Monkeys spend a huge part of their time hugging and grooming each other, so those born during this time enjoy being coddled, in love and also within their families. They can also be great protective parents for their children.

Falcon - Coz - Intellect

February 8th to March 8th

The Mexican Falcon is a native of North America. Its location ranges from the western provinces of Canada to Mexico. It nests in southern Canada, the United States, and northern Mexico.

Among the variety of Falcon that exist, three were found in the territories of the Mayan culture in ancient times; the most prevalent was The Guaco, also called the Laughing Falcon. There was also the Snake Hawk, called *Coz* in the Mayan language.

It is characterized mainly by its thin and pointed wings, which allow it to reach extremely high speeds. Peregrine Falcons are the fastest animals on the planet, reaching speeds in dive between 230 and 360 km/hour. In horizontal flight, it reaches 96 km/h.

It is a bird that flies high and locates its prey from above. Since it is a diurnal bird, it has a highly developed sense of sight. It is a great hunter and part of its diet is Snakes and Rabbits, as well as small birds it kills and shreds with its sharp claws and beak. They generally live in temperate and tropical zones and are sedentary.

A male Falcon, usually smaller than a female, can be distinguished from afar by its grayish hue on the head and the edges of the wings. They do not group except when they migrate, but they prefer to fly alone or in solitary pairs. They are capable of demonstrating great self-trust and self- reliance, which is their default inclination.

Flowers of the Month

The *Coz* period covers two solar months in the Mayan calendar. The first is known as *Yax*, which means clarity, and it is when the amount of light increases again and the days lengthen. The second month is called *Zac*, which means white, and it is when the flower of the region, the "toothleaf goldeneye" blooms. These flowers have a milky bud, highly valued because it provides nectar to bees, which they collect to eat. Then the nectar stored becomes a distinct honey, considered especially tasty. These two periods emphasize a time to achieve clarity and a time for manifestation.

Sign Traits

★ Those born between February 8 and March 8 are protected by the Falcon, a hunter bird, which helps them reach extraordinary intellectual and spiritual heights. Whether they use these gifts professionally or personally is up to them, but they do have the potential to become widely known for the way they stand out as special in some way.

★ They are people with a great sense of reality and a clear vision regarding the decisions to be made in life. These 2 qualities go well together, allowing them to manifest and make real that which they hope for. This rare quality, grounded expectations and wild dreams, make them consistent achievers in their own right. They are good strategists and even through most unlikely plans have a chance of success.

★ Falcon people have a great intuition to know what the future holds. They can use this within a system of divination, for example through cultivating skills as an astrologer or tarot reader. They would likely have a knack for such tools. This gift of intuition can also be used for professional gains and business success.

★ They are of intellectual tendencies and react when their ideas are threatened. Usually their ideas are outstanding, but they may need to develop strong social skills as well. Without intending to, their forthright character can bring challenges to some of their ideas, making it hard to get forge alliances that could be useful. One they do forge business contacts, they are honest and faithful to agreements made and the people behind them.

★ They have instinctive contact with higher intellectual powers. Whether they are understood as cultivated gifts or inherent gifts, there is an almost intuitive way in which they are able to put engage in intellectual pursuits.

★ They are intellectual and creative people, but they have difficulties to adapt to life. A part of this is rooted in their natural inclination to spend time alone. Another factor that can be challenging is that they sometimes lack a depth of understanding in the nuances of human relationships. For all this, when they do forge meaningful connections, they cherish the people around them.

★ They can link states of consciousness, heaven, and earth. Falcons observe from above, so people born under this sign see life from higher perspectives. Taking the path of spirituality is natural to them. They are able to intellectualize their spiritual values, and merge them with emotional conviction.

★ The Falcon's challenge is to ground their ideas to their daily plans. To ensure they are living a balanced life, not completely goal driven, so that they enjoy life as it comes. Plans might not always pan out the way they'd like it to, and yet they can still enjoy the journey.

Message

Your intellectual and spiritual gifts have the ability to inspire and help many people in life. You will need to cultivate kindness and patience towards yourself, as you learn to cultivate these attributes as skills, to be tapped into and strengthened. You are resilient and can be self-sufficient as a default position, but life takes on deeper richness and meaning as you connect with others. The best way to move towards alliances with others is by sharing your gifts and shining bright in the truth of who you are. You come to learn that you can depend on others.

In Love

Falcon people like to be happy. They also like to be cheerful, and they also enjoy sharing their vision and having their partner reach their levels of understanding, whether that be personal, emotional, or intellectual. They are happiest with people who feel safe enough to share their dreams with. They want someone, with whom they can share their wildest plans, and yet feel they are taken completely seriously. Their most outlandish plans feel more real when they have someone who believes in their ability to manifest them. They also like to be cheerful. They also enjoy sharing their vision, and having their partner reach their levels of understanding.

Falcons might have a hard time committing to a single person. However, when they do, it is usually for life, especially if their partner satisfies their intellectual needs. in fact, they are especially likely to fall in love with someone they consider to be a very good friend, and will choose to be dedicated to those who satisfy them intellectually. They do enjoy physical contact and affection, but until they know they have intellectual connection with the one they desire, they might choose not to spend the entire night.

Jaguar - Balam - Protector

March 9th to April 5th

The Jaguar is a carnivore feline in the Panthera genus. Only one of the four surviving species is found in the Americas. It is also the largest feline in the Americas, and the third largest in the world, after the tiger and the lion.

They have a robust and muscular frame, with significant variations in size. The weight of an adult can range between 45 and 130 kilograms. As in other species of mammals, females are usually slightly smaller than males. Their length from the nose to the tip of the tail can range from 1.70 meters to 2.50 meters. Their height is about 70 centimeters. The *Balam*'s head is big, with a prominent jaw. The color of their eyes varies from a golden yellow tone to a greenish yellow, and their ears are small and rounded.

Behavior

Jaguars have a life span of 20 years. They are primarily loners, ambush hunters, and clever in choosing prey. They are alpha predators, sitting on top of the food chain in their natural environment. Jaguars play an important role in stabilizing the ecosystems where they live by regulating entire populations of those species they feed on.

Jaguars have an exceptionally powerful bite, even compared to other big cats, allowing them to pierce the shells of certain reptiles, such as Turtles. They use an unusual method of killing. Jaguars will directly attack the head of their prey between the ears, with a lethal bite piercing through the skull. The Jaguars fangs can reach right into the brain of their prey.

The Worshipped Jaguars

For the Mayan civilization, Jaguars were the mediators between the living and the dead. They were powerful companions in the spiritual world. Whether as a symbol themselves, or as companions on the journey, it was the Jaguar that was looked to for spiritual guidance, assistance, and power.

The Mayan word for Jaguar is *Balam*, which was also included in the names of several Mayan kings. They kings would wear the head of their spirit animal on their heads, creating an association between them and the kind of the Mayan jungles, in the hearts and minds of their people. Jaguars were seen as great protectors, serving as emblems within the royal palaces, throughout the ancient civilization.

The Jaguar, or *Balam,* was also represented by the Mayans in buildings of their warriors. The places where soldiers frequented were often filled within images and symbols of the Jaguar. Jaguars were revered for their strength and particular way of attacking their prey. These were personal qualities looked to as the warriors' inspiration.

There were many sacred sites, temples, and ancient cities decorated with emblem of the Jaguar. In the Mayan city of *Chichén Itzá*, they built the "Temples of the Jaguar" next to the ball courts. The ancient city also held "The Platform of Eagles and Jaguars" and the "Throne of Kukulkán", shaped like this feline. Also, in the two ball courts found in *Cobá*, we can find reliefs with Jaguar figures. Other Mayan cities with representations of Jaguars include, but are not limited to, *Yaxchilán*, *Ek Balam*, and *Toniná*.

The ritual of the Jaguar was perhaps the best known among the Mayans, and it was celebrated along with the celebration of the descent of the Snake from heaven to fertilize the earth. The priests prepared the offerings and the celebration. To this day, thousands of people gather at the main pyramid of *Chichén Itzá* every Spiring Equinox, at the height of Jaguar month, to watch the light-and-shadow effect that forms 13 triangles in the north roof of the Palace.

Sign Traits

★ Those born under the sign of the Jaguar, from March 9 to April 5, usually display a leadership archetype. They are confident that, with strength and determination, their right actions will lead them to good results.

★ Like this feline, people with the spirit of the *Balam* are guided by tenacity and untamed courage. The key to their success, personal and professional, comes with age. It is as they grow in experience, that they learn their own unique way to directing this tremendous personal power, while honoring its' innate will quality.

★ Those born under the sign of the Jaguar are usually patient. They know how to act at the right moment. They may seem serene and unaffected on the surface, but something within always keeps focus on the most important priorities. Their attention towards preparation allows them to remain ready to act when the moment of opportunity presents itself.

★ Certainty might be the Jaguar's best attribute. They hold a confidence that isn't always quiet, as they will be blatant with it as needed in a given moment. In fact, the presentation of confidence can sometimes be a performance, when they feel they have to "act as if." The show often has the desired affect, from making them feel stronger or, at times, psyching out perceived opponents.

★ Jaguars are dedicated and studious workers. While the intellect can be a strength, they often have manual skills that they can utilize to their advantage. Whether this involves strong hand-eye coordination, ability in sports, or physical prowess on the dance floor. They enjoy activities that bring together mind and body.

★ Jaguar people might plan their life carefully. They are wise, and carefully weigh all the factors involved when deciding. While the Jaguar is known for their physical strength and prowess, they can also be highly strategic. They observe and weight all probabilities carefully. However, they might decide in an instant to pounce. In moments of decisive action, they are determined and unstoppable.

★ The Mayans thought of the Jaguar as the guardian of the high values of life. This was likely because Jaguars demonstrated keen skills and wisdom. The Jaguar person can master different arts, and demonstrate that some of the skills they develop are not only for practical application, but for intrinsic enjoyment as well.

★ Jaguar people can be temperamental at times, which can cause conflicts in their work or personal relationships. Their awakened instincts guide them to improve their life and the life of others. They have intellectual faculties that need to be worked hard, but can become exceptional. They like to show their accomplishments and their understanding of life. They are lucky in financial matters.

Message

You are someone with great courage, though it make take times of stress to make your appreciate this intrinsic gift. One area that gumption and bravery most make themselves known is when you feel the call to protect your loved ones, as the Jaguars take care of their cubs. Some of your greatest gains will come a period of solitude, and your greatest leaps forward in life will come after a time of meditative contemplation. Be patient with yourself in the downtimes. They might look calm or boring on the surface, but that is when wisdom is under process of integration. Your abilities are those that can shine very bright, crowning you as royalty in a least one area of life. Part of your meditation in life might be on deciding the types of activities you want and feel called to be good at. Once you realize where your gifts are, your cultivation might take time behind the scenes, but once you hit the stage, you are undeniable.

In Love

Jaguar people are usually detached, being playful in flirtations and in romantic dalliances. They might respond especially favorably to compliments, and even flattery. Though they might return flirtatious gestures, they might do so out of the thrill of the dance, and not because they hold genuine interest.

You will know when they are serious in their affections, when they share their boldest ambitions, looking to their potential partners for validation. They want someone who consistently tells them they are born to greatness, that they are special. Once they give of themselves, their displays of love can be bold. They are outspoken in and about their relationships. When they care, they will let their partner and the world know it.

Jaguars usually walk in pairs. They are very protective of their cubs, and they may even attack to defend them. Another trait, although contradictory, is that they like to be lonely and are territorial. Their challenge in relationships is to master their strength and divide the attention between their partner and their own goals.

Dog - Pek - Loyalty

April 6th to May 3rd

The *Xoloitzcuintle* is dog breed native to Mexico, distinct as one of the few hairless breeds in the world. It is known for its close relationship with Mexican culture. These dogs have a great historical, cultural and biological value. Their small numbers compared to other breeds, and their behavior, marked the *Xoloitzcuintle, also called* Pek, as sacred to the Mayans.

There is another type that has hair. Those born with hair are still considered a pure *Xoloitzcuintle* breed, and if they mate with a hairless one, they will have hairless pups. One litter can have both types of puppies. Some other cultures adopted this dog. These dogs are grouped by sizes: breed standard, medium, and miniature. The two biggest sizes stand out as guardian dogs, while the miniature size as a companion dog.

This breed of dog became especially linked to these moments of transition, from life to death, and from death to the afterlife. The *Pek* always was a companion during travels, in this world and in others. This trait extended beyond the end of life, as it was thought they escorted us through other realms, once we moved on from this lifetime. When someone became ill and died, dogs howled in sadness, which was thought to be part of their sacred pact, serving as evidence of their special abilities to see death.

The Pek In The Dresden Codex

On page 7 of the Dresden Codex, we find three figures that represent the ideas of loyalty, perseverance and eternity so treasured by the Mayans. In the first box, we see Mercury, *Ek Chuah*, following the Sun with a loyal heart. In the middle, we find the constellation of *Pek*—the dog—followed by *Ain Ek*, Saturn, "the eye of the alligator". In fact, this planet is the slowest of all those that can be seen with the naked eye, and it is related to the perseverance and eternity of its walk in the sky, just as *Pek* was a companion to men in their transit through life and death, and beyond.

Another representation of the constellation of the Dog can be found on page 15 of the same Codex, where it can be seen looking straight ahead and upwards to Sirius as it happens in the sky. Even in the adjoining image on the next page, the dog can be seen carried by the Milky Way to show that this constellation is ahead.

The sign of the Dog means honesty, guidance, loyalty, fidelity to friends, and the power of love. On page 21, we see it facing the Moon with all its symbolic figures. On page 30, we see how it goes upside down when the hot weather ends, to give way to *Kan*, marking thus the beginning of the rainy season. This is reinforced pages ahead, where we can see the dog descending from the sky holding torches, matching with the month *Kankin*, the Yellow Sun, wise and ready to give way to the sowing season.

Sign Traits

★ The sign of the *Pek* belongs to those born between April 6 and May 3. They are loyal, spiritual, protective, and generous. Dogs are domesticated animals and remain dependent on humans. They are their faithful companions and fierce guardians. They are great walkers and helpers, and warn of the dangers that can happen on the way. Similarly, those born under the sign of the Dog understand the interdependence we have on each other. They are faithful friends, fierce protectors, and genuinely social. They care about the people, who they share their time with.

★ Dogs are animals with a great sense of smell and intuition. Dogs can smell more than 10 000 times more acutely than humans. This is symbolic of the Dogs ability to perceive other dimensions. Dog people are experts at discovering feelings. In sometimes uncanny ways, they have a sense for what the people around them is feeling.

★ Dog people are exceptionally good friends, and they are notably loyal, especially in platonic alliances. This tendency can show in personal connections, but in business relationships as well. They are spiritual, generous protectors of those around them, having a near mystical sense of what another might need to feel 'safe'. They create environments that provide safety to all those who enter, and might use this skill towards their business success.

★ Dog people are protective and loving with their children, and with anyone they perceive as innocent. They will champion the underdog, whether that is in a spontaneous moment, or more formally through social action. They will always fight for those they think could use a helping hand.

★ The Dog person's strong instincts to possess, and with their inclination towards being territorial, they can be difficult to deal with at times. When they come out of their shell, they become audacious adventurers, making friends with the world. Locally, they might get involved in community projects, and in the process forge meaningful connections with those around them.

★ Dog people like to store and prepare for the future, although sometimes they can be detached and with little interest in things that others consider important. They might appear anxious at times, but this energy can be channeled to create artistic pieces, that make them proud.

★ *Xoloitzcuintles* huddle and stoically accompany their owners, until they perceive they have recovered. The company is even known to help with rheumatism relief, for example. Therefore, those born during this period know how to be with their sick relatives, sharing their presence and joy until they see them recover.

Message

Your life path is not one where you have to ever be alone. There are many genuine people, who want to know what an exchange of friendship is like. With them you can build community and bonds that last a lifetime. While you might be entrusted to guide people at times through their difficult transitions, you can't be responsible for the personal choices they make, nor should you be attached to them. People will make choices for many reasons that have nothing to do with you. Can you stay in the moment and exchange heartfelt friendship, even if their actions don't live up to your expectations? Of course you can, especially when you prioritize joy and play in as many moments as possible. Then, the transitions you help people through become bonafide moments of bonding, that change all involved for the better.

In Love

Dog folks are affectionate, playful, and inclined to fall in love. They have very active sexual instincts. However, they are able to separate physical expression and emotional entanglement. They can be cautious and watchful of their feelings.

Dog people are inclined to show off to attract the attention of a potential partner, and can get very territorial with them. However, if their partners are strong and demonstrate the ability to be a genuine companion to them, Dog folks are inclined to reach out and count on them. They can be loyal as friends, but not always loyal in love. They have a tendency to change partners. Some might even be inclined to insist on open relationships. It is friendship that inclines them to feelings of loyalty and fidelity. Being honest is the key to navigating changing alliances with integrity.

The quality of the Dog person's relationships will be determined by the degree of dedication they are capable of. The strength and ability of their partners to guide them, to build loyalty in the relationship through friendship and over time, while not feeling like they are solely responsible for the outcome, is the only true pathway to forge a path of love with the Dog.

Compatibility

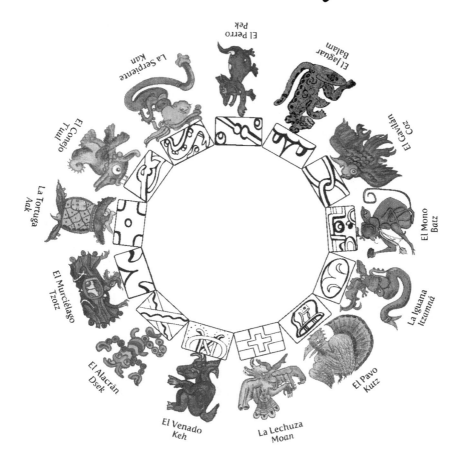

In this chapter, we will explain how the Mayan view of the sky can give us more tools to better acknowledge who we are in relation to others, and what are the characteristics that we must incorporate to complete our understanding of life.

The Mayan Zodiac suggests that, from the beginning of time, the gods themselves established that the behavior of the animals of the region offered some lessons and challenges. To overcome these challenges, we needed to cultivate a relationship with other animals, and incorporate all the qualities of the Zodiac. We can easily relate to the attribute of the 2 signs before and after our birth sign, since they share behavioral traits. As they move away from the birth sign, conscious and personal efforts then count to improve our character and who we are.

The Mayans were accomplished observers of nature. They took out from each process and relationship, whether in the sky or on earth, a model of behavior, an explanation, and a philosophy that gave meaning and order to each act and life circumstances.

In the sacred Mayan book, The *Popol Vuh*, the central part narrates the path of integration every human being has to follow to overcome their own darkness and reach their light. For the Mayans, life was a journey of fellowship, and of people who support each other in a lasting alliance, that brings success. Learning the different qualities life holds, while seeking their own personal improvement, was the key to this desired, happy state.

If we transfer this heroic and ancestral effort to our life conditions, and we learn to interact with others as family, partners, friends, or society, then we can consider the compatibility between the Mayan Zodiac signs. This compatibility responds, on the one hand, to their order, but also to the similar or contradictory traits between the signs. The two signs that follow our birth sign, before and after, share character and behavioral traits. The signs that are in the opposite part of the Zodiac also have traits that must be incorporated into life.

Snake, Kan

Those born under the sign of the Snake are consistent in their relationships, hence they might be demanding and jealous. They need gentle and sensitive partners. They are sensual and territorial regarding love. They are very generous people, that know how to guide their acquaintances and associates, since they know how to pay attention and listen. However, they usually justify their infidelities, and they can handle being in two relationships.

So those born under the Snake share with the previous two signs the dog's loyalty and the Jaguar's strength of love, except that those signs will encourage their territoriality and possessiveness. With the two following signs, the Snake shares creativity and fertility. With the Rabbit, they are encouraging excessive engagement in pleasure, which could weaken them. With the Turtle, they share similar emotional cadences, as well as the love for history and its cycles.

The Snake must battle the Falcon, their natural enemy, to be able to understand the intellectual heights and superior knowledge, achieving double rewards for their lives. Their relationship with the Bat shall provide them with the ability to see beyond earthly rewards, to complete their great knowledge.

Incorporating the Monkey's physical skills and mobility shall give the Snake more resources to unfold their practical sense. On the other hand, with the Scorpion, they will find a direct request for service and dedication.

With the Alligator Gar, the Snake will share their ability to not become corrupted, no matter how toxic the environment may be. Hopefully, they will also learn from their commitment skills. With the Deer, they will learn to share their knowledge in a more comprehensive way.

With a stronger will, they shall balance the love for socializing of the Turkey , along with the knowledge of the Owl, since being able to observe completely around them, could only reward them even more.

The snake and its sign was cherished, to the point of reverence, by the Mayans and all Mesoamerica. Any compatibility will take into account this inherent awareness of the Snake's own sacredness.

Rabbit, Túul

The Rabbit might seem to be the most idiosyncratic animal of the Zodiac. Being born during the expected rain season brings them a certain unpredictable love for celebration. However, its qualities are the loyalty of the dog and the ability to renew life, proof of this is their incredible reproductive capacity.

From the Turtle, the Rabbit must integrate the ability to be agile when needed, and retrace its steps. On the other hand, it is easy for Rabbit people to include the community or group into their well-being. As the Bat, their extraordinary hearing sense keeps them safe most of the times.

With the Jaguar, the Rabbit shares the ability to observe, especially that considered forbidden or dirty, as well as stealth to be attentive. With the Scorpion, they share the ability to be hidden, to come out when necessary, and being able to provide for their own.

It is more challenging for the Rabbit to take the Falcon's aim in, since they are their natural enemy. The Owl's acuity can be challenging for the Rabbit, as they could feel as if they could become easy prey. They also don't like to show off or hide out, like the Alligator Gar.

The Rabbit is inherently joyous and agile, and would need a partner with a sense of spontaneity, to keep the journey light and fun.

Turtle, Aak

The gift of the Turtle is to navigate in life, forming a path to which it can return as many times as needed. They have the support of the group through the example of the Bat, who teaches with their ability to multiply. The Turtle then gives birth to children like the Rabbit. Those born under the sign of the Turtle continue the Rabbit's example. They also know how to be independent, but sociable when demanded.

The Turtle knows the rhythmic and cyclical walk of the Snake will bring them the same wisdom they will share as medicine with their Scorpion sign siblings.

From the Dog, the Turtle must learn how to be loyal, which is the essence of this animal, but they have to avoid circling around so they can embark on a path towards light, which will eventually return them to their birthplace, but enriched and wiser.

Turtles don't stop when breeding. They actually continue their journey alone like the Deer, but like the Deer they must gather and share this knowledge later in life. On the other hand, it will be necessary for them not to hide themselves or their knowledge, like the Scorpion, because others need them as a guide.

The Turtle knows how to walk like the Sun, in the light. From there, they observe and know everything. The Jaguar is their counterpart in this sense because they observe at night and the stars are the ones that guide them. For the Turtle, their goal is to walk back with their stories and life experiences.

The Falcon and the Owl come to be their natural enemies that can take them by surprise, so they must incorporate being alert, and also being able to innovate in their walk, to assimilate the blessings they receive giving them a general sense, order and direction. On the other hand, the Turkey will teach them to show themselves and have confidence.

The Alligator Gar will teach the Turtle how to survive in the most difficult circumstances, and how it is important to go out from time to time to breathe the pure and the clean. They share with this extraordinary being the quality to use moderation or quickness as needed.

Bat, Zoots

Bats balance themselves with Falcons, since both know how to fly long distances, although Falcons hide at sunset just when the Bats go out with their group to look for food, water and adventures. Falcons do it alone or in pairs, never in a group.

With the Turtle, the Bat shares the pleasure of leaving and returning home. With the Rabbit, they share their reproductive capacity and group thinking. The Rabbit teaches the Bat to connect with water and find reservoirs of this precious liquid.

They must integrate the relationship with the cycles of the Snake, so they can understand the meaning of their existence beyond food and survival. Being wiser in the cycles of life is what both could learn.

Bats leave behind the waiting and chasing of the Scorpion, as well as the nervousness of the Deer that flees. However, both Bats and Deers are masters of the senses, because the Bats use sound to sense their surroundings, while the Deer do it through their smell.

With the Owl and the Deer, they share the love and trust of the dark. However, it is difficult to share traits with the Turkey, because showing off is not their thing. Due to their own characteristics, they prefer dim light, where they can share with their group without being too revealing.

Taking care of their own is a quality that brings the Bat closer with Dogs and Deer, sharing the loyalty for those they consider part of their pack.

They share night vision with the Jaguar and the Owl. What they bring out from what's hidden is what they can share with others. They also know how to wait for the right moment to move and get what they need.

With the Alligator Gar, they share the ability to take advantage of what is useful to them, but unlike the Gar, that waits for things to reach, Bats go out to find what they need. However, it may be wise to learn to see and take advantage of what arises.

Scorpion, Dsek

Scorpions hunt by day and try not to disturb anyone. They share the love for the dark with the Bat and the Deer, but are less friendly. However, their place in the Zodiac forces them to learn to seek the common good and what's important for the group.

The Scorpion person is more harmonious when they maintain a connection with their individualistic character, just like the Turtle and the Turkey . As the Turtle, they trust their children to find their own way, and like the Turkey , thinking about themselves is essential. Although the truth is, they don't like to be seen at all, much less to attract attention.

Scorpion folks must learn from the Turtle and the Owl, to share their experience and seek wisdom. Gaining a depth of understanding about what happens in their life is invaluable. Scorpion people could easily get stuck in repetitive thinking, and what's worse, in what injures them or makes them angry, unless they actively choose a path of cultivating wisdom.

It is difficult for the Scorpion to be as innocent and trusting as the Rabbit or the Turkey , but these are qualities that would make them enjoy life and social relationships more.

They find their balance with the Falcon, because just as the Falcon reaches heights, the Scorpion reaches depths, sharing this familiarity of the underworld with the Dog as well. However, they know that they must run away from the Snake and the Owl, as both would dominate them in an instant. Therefore, they must learn how to be alert and how to listen carefully. Scorpions not only know how to see at night, but to trust this unique ability is important to take care of themselves.

Scorpions in water resemble the attitude of the Alligator Gar that lurks in the dark, waiting for its prey to arrive. Both have the wisdom of those who have assimilated their darkness, but they must fight to get out of it and teach others to look for the light, instead of getting stuck in dead-end situations. This is precisely the lesson the Jaguar can share with them, knowing and understanding light, however dim it may seem.

Deer, Ceh

Deer people can learn to have balance with the Jaguar's temperament. Both animal signs know how to observe, but they respond in the opposite direction. The Deer runs away, while Jaguars attacks. Likewise in nature, the sweetness and gentleness of the Deer are desired by those born under the sign of the Jaguar, while the cunning and strength of this feline must be integrated by those born under the sign of the Deer.

Deer folks have the ability to be either alone or in a group, guiding them towards braveness, security and harmony, which they learned from the Scorpion and the Bat.

Deer people learn to be consistent and serious with the matters they teach, as the Owls, balancing them with the excitement and grace Turkey have. Deer folks learn how to share their stories and beauty, without being anxious, or insecure about being seen or applauded.

The Turtles and the Rabbits are as docile and gentle as the Deer. Between the three of them, they can make talent and grace multiply, creating stories and beautiful things.

It will be more difficult for Dear folks to integrate the stealth of the Snake and the Alligator Gar, because they make them anxious. However, they have to learn to reinvent, and not lose themselves in the frivolity and the superfluous, like the Snake. And as the

Alligator Gar, Deers need to immerse in the dark, to recognize the force of what's hidden and the occult.

With the Dog, they share loyalty to their group and the pleasure of captivating others. However, if they bring out their Falcon energy, they will enjoy their path without having to take care of themselves or show off to others.

Owl, Moan

The Owl has the gift to see at night like the Deer and the Scorpion. It can even better them, because they see almost at 360 degrees in the dark. Although they prefer to be in solitude as the Scorpion than social as the Deer, and even more than the Bat.

They reject attracting attention for its own sake, as opposed to the Turkey . Although going out and having fun do the Owl good, providing a break from strong emotions. The Owl can become like the Alligator Gar, lurking to catch their prey, when what they need is to go out and share their wisdom.

Owls don't need to reach the heights of the Falcon, because from where they are, they see what they need to see. However, it would do them good to recognize there is a broader perspective than what they perceive.

From the Turtle, The Owl learns to leave a mark. Those born under the sign of the Owl are not usually interested in making history. What interests them is what's hidden behind the obvious.

Their relationship with the Rabbit is difficult, because it is hard for them to assimilate their jokes. They share the predatory instinct and a taste for nocturnal activity with the Jaguar. They know how to move like the Jaguar and the Dog. However, the proximity to others is a task they must learn in life.

The Snake brings them balance. For the Mayans, the stellar position of the Owl announced death and the door to the underworld, while the Snake on its tail with the Pleiades announced the beginning of the sowing period and, therefore, of life.

Turkey, Kutz

Those born under the sign of the Turkey bring security and optimism to their relationships, but also a certain lack of commitment. This tendency might need to be evaluated at some point, so the relationship can keep going. On the positive side, this will be reflected as an ease to connect with others and by supporting the growth of people around them.

They share with the two previous signs, the Owl and the Deer, the ability to adapt and socialize. From the sign of the Alligator Gar and the Monkey, they will get the intelligence to ground their plans, and the skills and flexibility needed to be successful. However, they must disengage themselves from the seriousness and nervousness of the first two, and from the suspicion and fickleness of the Alligator Gar and the Monkey.

Those of the sign of the Turkey will find integration of the qualities of the signs of the Scorpion and the Falcon challenging, since the first one will question every movement they make, and the second will need a lot of socialization.

The Turkey could find the Bat and the Turtle hiding either in a cave or in their shell. That would not be tolerated by the Turkey. In addition, although that would give them a bit of calm and inner connection, they will find it difficult to contend with the strength and loyalty of the Jaguar, because they would force them to be more firm in their decisions.

Finally, as mirror and reflection, the Rabbit and the Snake oppose them. TheRabbit can attract them with the pleasures of having a good time. However, this can also challenge them, because that would suggest they have to put a limit, otherwise they would party all the time. With the Snake, they might find it hard to commit. They can develop their relationship calmly and patiently, or find it comes to a peaceful close. Being honest about their belief in the potential of a relationship could turn out to be a useful gift, for their own personal growth.

Alligator Gar, Xibcay

Those born under the sign of the Alligator Gar bring unmatched depth to their relationships. They like intense partners that resist their willpower and focus. Their love affairs are selective, but not scarce. They choose a partner to support them the way they feel they need. Their challenge is to open their heart with confidence and with the certainty they will receive love, just as all the other signs.

Gar folks will learn to give love without expecting to receive the exact proportion, and they will learn that love is given and is received according to their own willingness to receive it.
The Alligator Gar shares with the two previous signs the depth of the Owl and the certainty of knowing they are unique, like the Turkey . With the two later signs, they share the Monkey's ability for planning and the Falcon's fidelity. However, it is a bit more complex to incorporate the calmness of the Deer and the force of love of the Jaguar.

Now for those born under the sign of the Alligator Gar, incorporating the service capacity of the Scorpion would really be a gift, as well as the group conscience of the Bat. The Dog's capacity for enjoyment and gentleness, as well as the Snake's sensuality, would help them make important progress, because they tend to doubt the love they receive.

Finally, the opposite position of the Turtle and the Rabbit show the most important qualities to integrate, such as flowing with the feelings of others without getting overwhelmed, and learn not to dread small talk, chitchat and laughter.

Monkey, Batz

Those born under the sign of the Monkey bring to their relationships a high potential of sacrificing for the person they love, without becoming submissive. They fully enjoy cuddling, pampering and hugging their partners.

Their challenge is to overcome their fickle mindedness by avoiding distractions. On the other hand, their rationalization can lead them to be mere spectators of their life, without really taking risks or doing what they want.

With the two previous signs, Monkeys share the bonding of the Turkey and the Alligator Gar's observational skills. With the two later signs, they share the intellectual power of the Falcon, and the intensity of love of the Jaguar.

However, it will be more challenging for them to incorporate the breadth of vision and determination of the Owl into their beliefs. The restfulness of the Deer and the calmness of the Snake would give them serenity to make progress on their goals.

The Scorpion's ability to focus would balance their intellectual power with a willingness to serve. The Rabbit's lightness would alleviate their need to plan all their movements, although they have to be careful, because Rabbits may encourage their dispersion and fickleness.

In the opposite position, we find the Turtle. They have to learn patience from the Turtle, and how to avoid resentment. Finally, Monkeys must know that Bats are important, but not enough to lose themselves, since their creativity and individuality are the traits that will boost their self-esteem.

Falcon, Coz

Those born under the sign of the Falcon prefer committed, loving, and dedicated relationships that foster warmth. The kinder and warmer the partner, the more comfortable they will feel. However, they need a partner who inspires them and challenges their intellectual abilities. They fully enjoy pleasure, and must exercise their will so as not to give in to temptation. That is their challenge.

Those born with the Falcon as their sign share with the two previous signs the intelligence of the Monkey as well as the observational skills of the Alligator Gar. With the two later signs, they share the will and strength of the Jaguar and the loyalty of the Dog.

It is a bit more complex for the Falcon to incorporate the Turkey's socializing skills, or the wise calmness of the Snake. However, these two signs may open their souls to private introspection, that will inspire their social skills, and opening up in their encounters with others.

The wisdom of the Owl will be welcomed, because it would give them a breadth of consciousness. The meekness of the Rabbit will be helpful to them, learning to avoid taking criticism and opposition to their ideas too personally.

With the Deer, they will learn that the day can be enjoyed, without having to intellectualize everything excessively. The Turtle will teach them to connect with their feelings and go with the flow.

Finally, they learn from the Bat that caring for people is important. The Scorpion's ability to focus will help them display their amazing intellectual abilities, balancing them with the willingness to serve others.

Jaguar, Balam

People born under the Jaguar sign are detached, playful, and enjoy flattery. They are often bold and outspoken in their relationships. Usually, Jaguars walk in pairs. They bring value and strength of love to their relationships. Their challenge is to be careful, so that the expression of this feeling does not become aggressive or blind.

Therefore, people born under the Jaguar sign share with the two previous signs the intelligence of both the Falcon and the Monkey. That is how they master both their physical and intellectual knowledge. With the following two signs, they share the loyalty of the Dog, that allows them to defend their own, and the stillness of the Snake, to plan out their lives carefully.

It turns out to be a little more complicated for the Jaguar to incorporate the waiting ability of the Alligator Gar, as well as the lightness and submissiveness of the Rabbit, because it would allow them to mitigate their roughness or aggression.

It seems to be a bit more of a challenge to assimilate the love for socializing of the Turkey , which is something that would really benefit the Jaguar, strengthening their individual confidence. It would also be good for them to take in the wise stillness of the Owl, who can help the Jaguar be honest about their actions, and to know which steps are smart, and which are more risky.

Of the Turtle, the Jaguar shall learn from their tameness and patience, to flow along with their feelings. The same way they incorporate from the Bat the ability to run in groups, which would be an achievement for their lonely nature.

The most important gift the jaguar could receive would be from the Deer, which is to learn that there can be harmony between ideas, feelings and people. As well as from the Scorpion, which is to rescue the will to serve for the common good.

Dog, Pek

Those born under sign of the Dog are affectionate, playful and inclined to fall in love. However, they are wary and defensive with their feelings, since they take their time to show them. They like having their partner's attention, and are very territorial with them, meaning that they can be possessive and jealous if not careful.

Dog people share with the previous two signs the strength of love, both of the Jaguar and the Falcon, except that these signs will encourage their territorial needs. With the following two signs, they share the sensuality of the Snake, and the love for parties and life enjoyment of the Rabbit.

Incorporating the manual skills and mobility of the Monkey would provide the Dog with more resources, for them not to attach to just one profession. On the side of the Turtle, they could learn to share their feelings and not keep them to themselves like they normally do.

With the Alligator Gar, they will enjoy endless hours of exposure to the light and warmth of love. Hopefully, they will also learn from their commitment capacities. Along with the Bat, they will look after their tribes or clans with an impressive loyalty.

With a bigger willing effort, they shall balance the love to socialize of the Turkey , and incorporate the love for knowledge. On the other hand, incorporating the Scorpion's service ability will do them good, and would help them commit to noble causes.

The most important gift will be received from the Owl's wisdom, who spends the day observing. Dog people could learn to increase their visual skills, matching them up to their innate auditory gifts. Finally, with the Deer, they notice that knowledge achieved could also serve to improve oneself and the others, encouraging their understanding, and widening their sight.

Acknowledgments and Gratitudes

Yuriria's Gratitudes:

I thank the following people for their support in making this book.

To my parents for teaching me the passion to learn and study.

To my daughters for their encouragement and patience.

To my teachers, who have taught me and have shared their knowledge and wisdom.

To my fellow astrologers, who have listened to my essays with pleasure and interest.

To Nadiya Shah for her determined support and understanding.

To Benjamín González Roaro for his trust and support.

I am also grateful to the following scholars who inspired and guided me with their knowledge: Maria Luisa Kirchner de Miranda, Engr. Héctor M. Calderón, Lic. Marte Trejo, Bruce Scofield, Jose Antonio Lugo, Ursula Stockter, Nick Campion, Mtra. Wendy Ortiz, Gerardo Said, Alain and Lara Pavón.

Nadiya's Gratitudes:

Thank You to my Fabulous Friends, Fans, Superstars, Clients, and Students. Your trust means so much to me. Sharing this journey with you makes it that much more rewarding.

Thank you to my family, spiritual and physical. My amazing parents Shahnaz and Saif, my brother Fareed and Sister-In-Law Jenn. My many extended family members, especially my aunt Shireen Khan, whose wisdom shows up in my work almost every day.

My amazing team members Aida Gomez and Gilbert Escalier, as well as Miguel Gomez, Fiorella Alessandra Gonzalez Tornelli, Manuel Zaragoza, and Fernando Bastida. Thank You for being a part of the team that makes sure I am living my dreams.

I want to thank Yuriria herself, of course. She truly is one of the most brilliant people and insightful astrologers I know. Her friendship over the years has meant so much to me, and now to write this book with her, the first author other than myself on the Synchronicity Publications label. It truly is a dream come true on so many levels.

My amazing astrological community! My own personal Jupiter, Michael Barwick. The late, great Donna Van Toen, who I forever credit with my very first big breaks, placing me where I am today through the many blessings she granted me. There are many others in the astrology community who have my gratitude and love for all we share and all they give.

To the astrologers I meet at conferences or online, and to the many astrologers, who practice quietly at kitchen tables around the world. We are all part of one community. We are all family, and to you I send my most heartfelt gratitude and encouragement. It is a path of absolute dedication to a voice of inner authority within that leads us to this practice. As much as you give, as much as the rewards are there.

Credits

Códices:

The Codex Perez, Willard A. Theodore

Photographic facsimile, Bibliotheque Nationale, Paris, 1933

The Dresden Codex. Gates, William, Photographic facsimile. The Maya Society. Ed. Johns Hopkins University, 1932

El Códice Dresde, Thompson, Eric, FCE, 1972

Códice Madrid, Facsimilar, Museo de las Américas, Madrid.

Books:

Abreu Gómez, Ermilo. Popol Vuh, Antiguas Leyendas del Quiche

Ed. Oasis, México 1965

Aceves, Manuel. El Mexicano: Alquimia y Mito de Una Raza

Ed. Fontamara, México 1997.

Argüelles, José, El Factor Maya, Hoja Casa Editorial, México, 1992.

Aveni, Anthony. Conversing With the Planets. Ed. Kodansha International, U.S.A. 1994

Aveni, Anthony, Observadores del Cielo en el México Antiguo. FCE México, 2005.

Barbault, André, Astrología Mundial, Ed. Visión Libros, Barcelona, 1981.

Barrera Vázquez, A. y Rendón, Silvia. El Libro de los Libros de Chilam Balam, FCE, México, 2005.

Barrera Vazquez, A , Et. al. Diccionario Maya – Español,

Ed. Porrúa. México 1992.

Brady, Bernardette, Fixed Stars Ed. Samuel Weisser, Inc. U.S.A., 1998

Calderón, Héctor. Clave fonética de los Jeroglíficos Mayas. Ed. Orión México, 1962.

Calderón, Héctor. Los Mayas y los Eclipses, Grupo Dzíbil, México, 1991.

Calderón, Héctor. Correlación de la Rueda de Katunes: La Cuenta Larga y Las Fechas Cristianas.

Ed. Grupo Dzíbil, México 1982

Calderón, Héctor. Notas explicativas de la correlación de Katunes, la cuenta Larga y Las fechas Cristianas.

Cuaderno Dzíbil n° 2 Grupo Dzíbil, México 1982.

Calderón, Héctor. La Ciencia Matemática de los Mayas. Ed. Orión, México 1966

Campion Nick, Astrología Mundana, Ed. Aquarian Press, Great Britain, 1985.

Cañedo Gerardo, Misterios Mayas, Ed. Editores Mexicanos Unidos, 2009,

D. Coe Michael, El Desciframiento de los Glifos Mayas. FCE, México 2010

Escalante, Pablo Et. Al. Nueva Historia Mínima de México. Ed. El Colegio de México, México 2010.

Fernández, Felipe, La Cruz de Palenque, Freidel, David, et. Al. El cosmos Maya FCE, México,

1993.

Galena, Patricia Et. Al. El Nacimiento de México. FCE, México 1999.

Gómez Navarrete, Javier A. Método para el aprendizaje de la Lengua Maya,

1er curso "MAAYA T'AAN JUMP'EL" Quintana Roo, 2002.

Graham, Ian. Caligrafía Maya. Ed. La Vaca Independiente, México 1999

Gutiérrez Vivó, José, Et. Al. El Otro Yo del Mexicano. Ed. Océano, México 1998

Hammond, Norman. Ancient Maya Civilization. Ed. Cambridge University Press, USA 1982

Hand Clow, Barbara. El Código Maya. Ed. Grijalbo, México 2007

Harleston, Hugh. Prediction by Precalculation of Archelogical Sites, Ed. UAC-KAN research

Group, México 1984.

Hasselkus M., Hans. Estructura de la Glífica Maya. Ed. Hasselkus, México 1998.

Hasselkus Hans Wooh, Introducción al conocimiento de los Códices Mayas. Ed. Hasselkus,

México 1989.

Harleston, Hugh. El Zodiaco Maya. Su Horóscopo y Características Psíquicas. Ed. Diana, México,

1993.

Hoffman, Ebertin. Fixed Stars, Ed. AFA Inc. U.S.A. 1971.

Jelsrud Waldemar, Enigmas del Pasado. Acambaro, Gto. 1942.

Kettunen Harr, et. Al. Introducción a los Jeroglíficos Mayas. Manual para el Taller de Escritura 2° Ed. Universidad de Helsinki, 2004.

Kirchner y Campos, María Luisa. Tras la pista del Chilam Balam. Ed. Plenitud, México 2009

Krickeberg, Walter, Las antiguas culturas de México, FCE, 1961.

Lesur, Luis. Las Claves Ocultas de la Virgen de Guadalupe, Ed. Plaza Janéz, México, 2005.

Lesur, Luis. Vicios y Prejuicios de la Astrología, Ed. Plaza Janéz, México, 2003

Le Plongeon, August, Misterios de los mayas quiches. Ed. Medio Oriente, Barcelona 1933.

Luxton, Richard Balam, Pablo. Sueño del Camino Maya: El Chamanismo Ilustrado. FCE, México 1986.

Maciá Tito. Descifrando los Códices Mayas – 2012- Ed. Índigo, Barcelona, 2009

Magaloni Duarte, Ignacio, Educadores del Mundo, Ed. B.Costa - Amic, 1995

Milbrath Susan, Star Gods of The Maya. University of Press, USA, 1982.

Martínez del Sobral Margarita, Geometría Mesoamericana, FCE, México, 2000.

Martínez Paredes, Domingo, El Hombre y el Cosmos en el Mundo Maya

Cuadernos de Lectura Popular, México, 1970.

Martínez Paredes, Domingo, Diez Leyendas Maya. Ed. Manuel Porrúa S.A., México 1978

Martínez Paredes, Domingo, Psicotrónica de los mayas, Ed. Orión, México 1980

Martínez Paredes, Domingo, Traducción de los glifos mayas, cuaderno facsimilar de trabajo en taller, México 1982.

Morley, Sivanus, La Civilización Maya, FCE, México 1972.

Noriega, Raúl, Sabiduría Matemática, Astronómica y Cronológica. Ponencia facsimilar. México.

Nohol Chan Kín, Piña Chán Román, Arenas del Tiempo Recuperadas, Gobierno de Campeche, México, 1994.

Olivier, Guilhem. Tezcatlipoca, burlas y metamorfosis de un Dios azteca. FCE, México, 2004.

Ortiz, Fernando, El Huracán, FCE, México, 2005.

Pavón Abreú, Raúl, S. Morley, Cronología maya, Ayuntamiento de Campeche, 1985.

Martínez, Pérez, Héctor, Crónica Chac, Xulub Chén.

Perez Mejia, Rolando, Galván Hernández José, Diccionario Español - Quiché. Guatemala 2007.

Piña Chán, Beatriz de, Iconografía Mexicana III, Colección Cienitífica. INAH, 2002.

Piña Chán Román, Las culturas preclásicas de México, FCE, México 1955.

Piña Chan Román, Quetzalcóatl, Serpiente Emplumada. FCE, México, 1977.

Richardson, B. Gill. Las Grandes Sequías Mayas, FCE México, 2008.

Riva Palacio, Antonio y Alfredo Chavero, México a través de los siglos, Ed. Cumbres, México, 1979.

Robson, Viviane Las Estrellas Fijas y las Constelaciones. Ed. Sirio, España, 1988.

Rossi, Melissa. Decoding 2012. Ed. Chronicle Books, USA 2010

Schell, Rolfe. Album Maya, Ed. Island Press, USA 1973

Scofield, Bruce and Orr Barry, How to practice Mayan Astrology. Ed. Bear & Co. Vermont, 2007.

Solis Alcalá Ermilo Ed. Códice Pérez. Ediciones de la liga de Acción Social. Mérida Yucatán, México, 1949.

Sotelo Santos, Laura Elena. Las Ideas Cosmológicas Mayas en el Siglo XVI, Ed. UNAM, México 1988.

Stephens, John L. y Catherwood Frederick, Incidencias de Viaje a Yucatán, Ed. Panorama, México, 1980.

Sprajc, Ivan. La Estrella de Quetzalcóatl: La Estrella Venus en Mesoamérica. Ed. Diana, México 1996.

Sten, María. Las Extraordinarias Historias de los Códices Mexicanos. Ed. Joaquín Mortiz, México 1978.

Thompson, Eric. Catalog of Maya Hieroglyphs, University of Oklahoma Press, 1976.

Thompson, Eric J, Grandeza y decadencia de los mayas, FCE, México, 1940

Thompson, Eric. Maya Hieroglyphs without Tears. British Museum Publications.

Great Britain, 1972.

Tibon, Gutierre. El Ombligo, Como Centro Cósmico. FCE, México, 2005.

Trejo Carrillo, Fernando y Sandoval Campos Ermilo, Historia de Campeche, Universidad Autónoma de Campeche, México 1985

Trejo Sandoval, Marte, Los Vórtices del Tiempo. Fundación Consejo Rescate de Tradiciones Cultura y Ecología S.C. México, 2001.

Trejo Sandoval, Marte, Las Ciudades del Cielo. Hoja Casa Editorial, México 1992

Von Hagen, Víctor, En busca de los mayas, Ed. Diana, México, 1969.

Magazines:

Arqueología Mexicana:

La pintura Maya, Vol XVI num. 93

Calendarios Prehispánicos, Vol VII num.41

Arqueoastronomía Mesoamericana, Vol VIII num.47

El Maíz, Edición especial 38

La escritura Maya Vol VIII num. 48

Augurios, profecías y pronósticos mayas. Vol. XVII num. 103.

Astronomy in the Ancient América, Robert Hicks en Sky & Telescope, 6 de junio 1976.

Estudios de la Cultura Maya, Vol XIX. UNAM, México 1992.

Books of Chilam Balam

Cantares de Dzibalché - Barrera Vázquez Alfredo, INAH, México 1965

Chilam Balam de Chumayel, Mediz Bolio Antonio, UNAM, México 1941.

Chilam Balam de Tuzik - Grupo Dzibil, México 1976

Códice Pérez - Solis Alcalá Hermilo, Imprenta Oriente, Mérida Yucatán, México 1949.

Manuscrito de Chán Cáh - Grupo Dzibil, México 1982.

Manuscrito de Tekax y Nah - Grupo Dzibil, México 1981.

French Vanity Fair named Nadiya Shah one of the top 12 astrologers on the planet, crowning her a pioneer in video astrology. She is an Internationally Syndicated Astrologer, Author, Media Personality, and is one of the few people in the world to hold an M.A. in the Cultural Study of Cosmology and Divination, from the University of Kent, United Kingdom.

Her last 3 books debuted as #1 New Releases in New Age Astrology on Amazon. Her School "Synchronicity University" teaches astrology and tarot worldwide. Nadiya's wildly popular Youtube channel, nadiyashahdotcom, is one of the most watched Astrology channels in the world.

Visit Nadiya's website at:

NadiyaShah.com

Yuriria Robles is an art historian with a master's degree in visual arts. She is also a Resonance Repatternig certified practitioner and teacher, and a NCGR IV certified astrologer.

Robles is the author of the books "Planetary Rituals" and "The Return of the Maya". She is also creator of the TV series "Mayan Horizons", which features a search on the Mayan zodiac relating it to archaeological sites. She gives lectures on Mayan Astrology and The Mayan Calendar.

She currently works in the National Lottery of Mexico that performs a Zodiac Draw permanently. She publishes weekly in writing and video predictions by signs and mundane views. An international presenter and consulting astrologer since 1988, Robles also presents her art in exhibitions around the world, as she continues to be inspired by astrology, fortune, and luck.

Find her online at

facebook.com/yuririastrologa

Printed in Poland
by Amazon Fulfillment
Poland Sp. z o.o., Wrocław